**TEACHER'S PET PUBLICATIONS**

PUZZLE PACK
for
Scorpions

based on the book by
Walter Dean Myers

Written by
Mary B. Collins

© 2005 Teacher's Pet Publications
All Rights Reserved

The materials in this packet are copyrighted
by Teacher's Pet Publications, Inc.

These pages may be duplicated by the purchaser
for use in the purchaser's own classroom.

Copying any of these materials and distributing them
for any other purpose is a violation of the copyright laws.

© 2005 Teacher's Pet Publications, Inc.
www.tpet.com

INTRODUCTION

If you already own the LitPlan for this title, this Puzzle Pack will refresh your Unit Resource Materials and Vocabulary Resource Materials sections plus give you additional materials you can substitute into the tests. If you do not already have a complete LitPlan, these pages will give you some supplemental materials to use with your own plan. There are two main groups of materials: one set for unit words (such as characters' names, symbols, places, etc.) and one set for vocabulary words associated with the book.

WORD LIST

There is a word list for both the unit words and the vocabulary words. These lists show you which words are being used in the materials and the clues or definitions being used for those words. You may want to give students a word list with clues/definitions to help them, or you may want students to only have a word list (without clues/definitions) if you want them to work a little harder. Both are available for duplication. The word lists can also be your "calling key" for the bingo games.

FILL IN THE BLANK AND MATCHING

There are 4 each of the fill in the blank and matching worksheets for both the unit and vocabulary words. These pages can be used either as extra worksheets for students or as objective parts of a unit test. They can be done individually if students need extra help or as a whole class activity to review the material covered.

MAGIC SQUARES

The magic squares not only reinforce the material covered but also work on reasoning and math skills. Many teachers have told us that their students really enjoy doing these!

WORD SEARCH PUZZLES

The word search words go in all directions, as indicated on your answer keys. Two of the word search puzzles have the clues listed rather than the words. This makes the puzzle a little more difficult, but it reinforces the material better. Two word search puzzles have words only for students who find the clue puzzles too difficult.

CROSSWORD PUZZLES

Both unit and vocabulary word sections have 4 crossword puzzles.

BINGO CARDS

There are 32 individual bingo cards for the unit words and 32 individual bingo cards for the vocabulary words. You can use your word list as a "call list," calling the words at random and marking them off of your list as you go, or you could use the flash cards by cutting them apart and drawing the words at random from a hat (or box or whatever). To make a better review, you might ask for the definition and spelling of each word as you call it out–or you could call out the definitions and have students tell you the words they need to look for on the puzzle.

JUGGLE LETTERS

The vocabulary juggle letter game is intended to help students learn the spellings of the words. One sheet has the definitions listed on it as an extra help for students who need it or to reinforce the definitions if you choose to do so.

FLASH CARDS

We've included a set of vocabulary flash cards you can duplicate, cut, and fold for your students. Some teachers make a few sets for general use by the class; others make a set for each student. Some teachers duplicate them for each student and have the students cut & fold their own. You can cut out just the words and put them in a hat, have each student pick out one word and write the definition and a sentence for that word. Students then swap words and papers, with the next student adding a sentence of his own under the last one. You can have students swap as many times as you like. Each time the student will read the sentences written prior to his own and then add a sentence. You can cut out the words and definitions separately and play "I Have; Who Has?" Each student in the room draws a word and definition. The first student says, "I have (the name of the word). Who has the definition?" The student with the definition reads it then says, "I have (the name of the vocabulary word she has). Who has the definition?" The round continues until all words and definitions have been given.

Scorpions Word List

No.	Word	Clue/Definition
1.	ABUELA	Tito's grandmother
2.	ADDISON	Mr. ____ was Randy's lawyer.
3.	ANGEL	Said Jamal didn't have any experience
4.	ASTHMA	Tito's ailment
5.	BLOOD	First to notice Jamal's gun
6.	BOATS	Jamal and Tito dreamed of owning them.
7.	BASIN	Boat ____; Jamal and Tito liked to visit this place.
8.	BROWN	Miss ____; Jamal's favorite teacher
9.	BURN	Mama's ailment
10.	CATHOLIC	Tito's religion
11.	CELIA	____ Rodriguez wanted to borrow fifteen cents from Jamal or Tito.
12.	DARNELL	Asked Jamal if he had a gun
13.	DAVIDSON	Mr. ____, principal; didn't notice when Jamal was on time
14.	DRAW	Jamal liked to ____ and paint.
15.	DRAWING	Jamal gave one of his to Tito when he left.
16.	DWAYNE	Jamal pulled the gun on him during a fight.
17.	EIGHT	Sassy's age
18.	FIREHOUSE	Scorpion's base was an old one
19.	FIVE	At first the lawyer wanted ____hundred dollars for the appeal.
20.	FOURTEEN	Angel's age
21.	GONZALEZ	Jamal worked in his bodega.
22.	GREEN	____ Haven; Randy was in prison there
23.	GUN	What Mack gave Jamal
24.	HARLEM	Setting of the novel
25.	HICKS	Mrs. ____ wondered what her family was coming to.
26.	INDIAN	Wondered if Jamal 'had the heart'
27.	WHALEY	Jerry ____; roughest kid in the school
28.	JEVON	____Hicks; told Jamal to act more like a young man
29.	MACK	Gave the gun to Jamal
30.	MARCUS	____Garvey; name of the park
31.	MITCHELL	Mrs. ____ told Dwayne to stay after school.
32.	MYRNA	Didn't like Dwayne; gave him a disgusted look
33.	OSWALDO	First name of boy who raced down the stairs in school with Jamal
34.	PUERTO	____ Rico; Tito went here after the fight
35.	RANDY	Jamal's older brother who was in jail
36.	BIGGS	Reverend ____; prayed with the family
37.	RICH	Mrs. ____asked Jamal if he would ever pay attention in class
38.	ROBERTS	Mrs. ____ gave peppermints to students.
39.	SCORPIONS	Randy used to be their leader.
40.	SEVENTEEN	Randy's age
41.	SEVENTH	Mrs. Rich said Jamal might spend another year in ____ grade.
42.	SINGH	Kids were sent to Mr. ____ if they were in trouble.
43.	SIXTEEN	Mack's age
44.	SPOFFORD	Prison where Mack had been
45.	STANTON	Mr. ____ would not loan Mama the money.
46.	TITO	____ Cruz; Jamal's best friend
47.	TWELVE	Jamal's age
48.	TWO	The lawyer wanted ____ thousand dollars for the appeal.
49.	VELASQUEZ	Last name of boy who raced down the stairs in school with Jamal
50.	WILLIE	Turned Randy in to a cop a plea.

Scorpions Fill In The Blanks 1

_____

_____

_____

_____

_____

_____

_____

_____

_____

_____

_____

_____

_____

_____

_____

_____

_____

_____

_____

_____

1. ____ Haven; Randy was in prison there
2. Didn't like Dwayne; gave him a disgusted look
3. First name of boy who raced down the stairs in school with Jamal
4. Mrs. Rich said Jamal might spend another year in ____ grade.
5. Last name of boy who raced down the stairs in school with Jamal
6. Randy's age
7. Sassy's age
8. Miss ____; Jamal's favorite teacher
9. Mrs. ____ gave peppermints to students.
10. Kids were sent to Mr. ____ if they were in trouble.
11. ____ Garvey; name of the park
12. Jamal gave one of his to Tito when he left.
13. Angel's age
14. Turned Randy in to a cop a plea.
15. Jerry ____; roughest kid in the school
16. Mr. ____, principal; didn't notice when Jamal was on time
17. Tito's religion
18. Wondered if Jamal 'had the heart'
19. Jamal and Tito dreamed of owning them.
20. Gave the gun to Jamal

Scorpions Fill In The Blanks 1 Answer Key

GREEN	1.	____ Haven; Randy was in prison there
MYRNA	2.	Didn't like Dwayne; gave him a disgusted look
OSWALDO	3.	First name of boy who raced down the stairs in school with Jamal
SEVENTH	4.	Mrs. Rich said Jamal might spend another year in ____ grade.
VELASQUEZ	5.	Last name of boy who raced down the stairs in school with Jamal
SEVENTEEN	6.	Randy's age
EIGHT	7.	Sassy's age
BROWN	8.	Miss ____; Jamal's favorite teacher
ROBERTS	9.	Mrs. ____ gave peppermints to students.
SINGH	10.	Kids were sent to Mr. ____ if they were in trouble.
MARCUS	11.	____Garvey; name of the park
DRAWING	12.	Jamal gave one of his to Tito when he left.
FOURTEEN	13.	Angel's age
WILLIE	14.	Turned Randy in to a cop a plea.
WHALEY	15.	Jerry ____; roughest kid in the school
DAVIDSON	16.	Mr. ____, principal; didn't notice when Jamal was on time
CATHOLIC	17.	Tito's religion
INDIAN	18.	Wondered if Jamal 'had the heart'
BOATS	19.	Jamal and Tito dreamed of owning them.
MACK	20.	Gave the gun to Jamal

Scorpions Fill In The Blanks 2

_____ 1. Jamal's older brother who was in jail

_____ 2. Mack's age

_____ 3. Didn't like Dwayne; gave him a disgusted look

_____ 4. Jamal gave one of his to Tito when he left.

_____ 5. Jamal worked in his bodega.

_____ 6. Jerry ____; roughest kid in the school

_____ 7. Setting of the novel

_____ 8. ____Hicks; told Jamal to act more like a young man

_____ 9. Scorpion's base was an old one

_____ 10. Gave the gun to Jamal

_____ 11. Mr. ____ was Randy's lawyer.

_____ 12. Mama's ailment

_____ 13. Mr. ____, principal; didn't notice when Jamal was on time

_____ 14. Kids were sent to Mr. ____ if they were in trouble.

_____ 15. Mrs. Rich said Jamal might spend another year in ____ grade.

16. Randy used to be their leader.

_____ 17. Mrs. ____ wondered what her family was coming to.

_____ 18. Sassy's age

_____ 19. At first the lawyer wanted ____hundred dollars for the appeal.

20. Reverend ____; prayed with the family

Scorpions Fill In The Blanks 2 Answer Key

RANDY	1. Jamal's older brother who was in jail
SIXTEEN	2. Mack's age
MYRNA	3. Didn't like Dwayne; gave him a disgusted look
DRAWING	4. Jamal gave one of his to Tito when he left.
GONZALEZ	5. Jamal worked in his bodega.
WHALEY	6. Jerry ____; roughest kid in the school
HARLEM	7. Setting of the novel
JEVON	8. ____Hicks; told Jamal to act more like a young man
FIREHOUSE	9. Scorpion's base was an old one
MACK	10. Gave the gun to Jamal
ADDISON	11. Mr. ____ was Randy's lawyer.
BURN	12. Mama's ailment
DAVIDSON	13. Mr. ____, principal; didn't notice when Jamal was on time
SINGH	14. Kids were sent to Mr. ____ if they were in trouble.
SEVENTH	15. Mrs. Rich said Jamal might spend another year in ____ grade.
SCORPIONS	16. Randy used to be their leader.
HICKS	17. Mrs. ____ wondered what her family was coming to.
EIGHT	18. Sassy's age
FIVE	19. At first the lawyer wanted ____hundred dollars for the appeal.
BIGGS	20. Reverend ____; prayed with the family

Scorpions Fill In The Blanks 3

1. At first the lawyer wanted ____ hundred dollars for the appeal.
2. Kids were sent to Mr. ____ if they were in trouble.
3. Wondered if Jamal 'had the heart'
4. What Mack gave Jamal
5. Angel's age
6. Jamal gave one of his to Tito when he left.
7. Tito's grandmother
8. ____ Rodriguez wanted to borrow fifteen cents from Jamal or Tito.
9. Gave the gun to Jamal
10. Last name of boy who raced down the stairs in school with Jamal
11. Mr. ____ would not loan Mama the money.
12. Randy's age
13. ____ Garvey; name of the park
14. ____ Haven; Randy was in prison there
15. ____ Rico; Tito went here after the fight
16. Randy used to be their leader.
17. Mack's age
18. Boat ____; Jamal and Tito liked to visit this place.
19. Reverend ____; prayed with the family
20. Mrs. ____ wondered what her family was coming to.

Scorpions Fill In The Blanks 3 Answer Key

FIVE	1. At first the lawyer wanted ____ hundred dollars for the appeal.
SINGH	2. Kids were sent to Mr. ____ if they were in trouble.
INDIAN	3. Wondered if Jamal 'had the heart'
GUN	4. What Mack gave Jamal
FOURTEEN	5. Angel's age
DRAWING	6. Jamal gave one of his to Tito when he left.
ABUELA	7. Tito's grandmother
CELIA	8. ____ Rodriguez wanted to borrow fifteen cents from Jamal or Tito.
MACK	9. Gave the gun to Jamal
VELASQUEZ	10. Last name of boy who raced down the stairs in school with Jamal
STANTON	11. Mr. ____ would not loan Mama the money.
SEVENTEEN	12. Randy's age
MARCUS	13. ____ Garvey; name of the park
GREEN	14. ____ Haven; Randy was in prison there
PUERTO	15. ____ Rico; Tito went here after the fight
SCORPIONS	16. Randy used to be their leader.
SIXTEEN	17. Mack's age
BASIN	18. Boat ____; Jamal and Tito liked to visit this place.
BIGGS	19. Reverend ____; prayed with the family
HICKS	20. Mrs. ____ wondered what her family was coming to.

Scorpions Fill In The Blanks 4

_____

_____

_____

_____

_____

_____

_____

_____

_____

_____

_____

_____

_____

_____

_____

_____

_____

_____

_____

_____

1. Mr. _____ was Randy's lawyer.
2. Turned Randy in to a cop a plea.
3. Setting of the novel
4. Mrs. _____ told Dwayne to stay after school.
5. Miss _____; Jamal's favorite teacher
6. Randy's age
7. _____ Haven; Randy was in prison there
8. Jamal's older brother who was in jail
9. Mr. _____ would not loan Mama the money.
10. Wondered if Jamal 'had the heart'
11. Angel's age
12. Mrs. _____ gave peppermints to students.
13. _____ Rico; Tito went here after the fight
14. First name of boy who raced down the stairs in school with Jamal
15. Kids were sent to Mr. _____ if they were in trouble.
16. Jamal pulled the gun on him during a fight.
17. Mrs. _____ asked Jamal if he would ever pay attention in class
18. Randy used to be their leader.
19. _____ Cruz; Jamal's best friend
20. Jamal worked in his bodega.

Scorpions Fill In The Blanks 4 Answer Key

ADDISON	1. Mr. ____ was Randy's lawyer.
WILLIE	2. Turned Randy in to a cop a plea.
HARLEM	3. Setting of the novel
MITCHELL	4. Mrs. ____ told Dwayne to stay after school.
BROWN	5. Miss ____; Jamal's favorite teacher
SEVENTEEN	6. Randy's age
GREEN	7. ____ Haven; Randy was in prison there
RANDY	8. Jamal's older brother who was in jail
STANTON	9. Mr. ____ would not loan Mama the money.
INDIAN	10. Wondered if Jamal 'had the heart'
FOURTEEN	11. Angel's age
ROBERTS	12. Mrs. ____ gave peppermints to students.
PUERTO	13. ____ Rico; Tito went here after the fight
OSWALDO	14. First name of boy who raced down the stairs in school with Jamal
SINGH	15. Kids were sent to Mr. ____ if they were in trouble.
DWAYNE	16. Jamal pulled the gun on him during a fight.
RICH	17. Mrs. ____ asked Jamal if he would ever pay attention in class
SCORPIONS	18. Randy used to be their leader.
TITO	19. ____ Cruz; Jamal's best friend
GONZALEZ	20. Jamal worked in his bodega.

Scorpions Matching 1

___ 1. FIREHOUSE   A. Setting of the novel
___ 2. MITCHELL   B. Reverend ____; prayed with the family
___ 3. GREEN   C. ____ Haven; Randy was in prison there
___ 4. SEVENTEEN   D. Tito's ailment
___ 5. PUERTO   E. What Mack gave Jamal
___ 6. TWO   F. Jamal gave one of his to Tito when he left.
___ 7. DAVIDSON   G. Mrs. ____ wondered what her family was coming to.
___ 8. SINGH   H. Scorpion's base was an old one
___ 9. TWELVE   I. Jamal's age
___ 10. GONZALEZ   J. Mrs. ____ told Dwayne to stay after school.
___ 11. GUN   K. At first the lawyer wanted ____ hundred dollars for the appeal.
___ 12. DRAWING   L. First name of boy who raced down the stairs in school with Jamal
___ 13. DWAYNE   M. The lawyer wanted ____ thousand dollars for the appeal.
___ 14. INDIAN   N. Randy's age
___ 15. HARLEM   O. Wondered if Jamal 'had the heart'
___ 16. WILLIE   P. ____ Hicks; told Jamal to act more like a young man
___ 17. BROWN   Q. Miss ____; Jamal's favorite teacher
___ 18. CELIA   R. Jamal worked in his bodega.
___ 19. ASTHMA   S. Jamal pulled the gun on him during a fight.
___ 20. HICKS   T. ____ Rodriguez wanted to borrow fifteen cents from Jamal or Tito.
___ 21. JEVON   U. Mr. ____, principal; didn't notice when Jamal was on time
___ 22. BIGGS   V. Turned Randy in to a cop a plea.
___ 23. BASIN   W. Boat ____; Jamal and Tito liked to visit this place.
___ 24. OSWALDO   X. Kids were sent to Mr. ____ if they were in trouble.
___ 25. FIVE   Y. ____ Rico; Tito went here after the fight

Scorpions Matching 1 Answer Key

H - 1. FIREHOUSE	A.	Setting of the novel
J - 2. MITCHELL	B.	Reverend ____; prayed with the family
C - 3. GREEN	C.	____ Haven; Randy was in prison there
N - 4. SEVENTEEN	D.	Tito's ailment
Y - 5. PUERTO	E.	What Mack gave Jamal
M - 6. TWO	F.	Jamal gave one of his to Tito when he left.
U - 7. DAVIDSON	G.	Mrs. ____ wondered what her family was coming to.
X - 8. SINGH	H.	Scorpion's base was an old one
I - 9. TWELVE	I.	Jamal's age
R - 10. GONZALEZ	J.	Mrs. ____ told Dwayne to stay after school.
E - 11. GUN	K.	At first the lawyer wanted ____ hundred dollars for the appeal.
F - 12. DRAWING	L.	First name of boy who raced down the stairs in school with Jamal
S - 13. DWAYNE	M.	The lawyer wanted ____ thousand dollars for the appeal.
O - 14. INDIAN	N.	Randy's age
A - 15. HARLEM	O.	Wondered if Jamal 'had the heart'
V - 16. WILLIE	P.	____ Hicks; told Jamal to act more like a young man
Q - 17. BROWN	Q.	Miss ____; Jamal's favorite teacher
T - 18. CELIA	R.	Jamal worked in his bodega.
D - 19. ASTHMA	S.	Jamal pulled the gun on him during a fight.
G - 20. HICKS	T.	____ Rodriguez wanted to borrow fifteen cents from Jamal or Tito.
P - 21. JEVON	U.	Mr. ____, principal; didn't notice when Jamal was on time
B - 22. BIGGS	V.	Turned Randy in to a cop a plea.
W - 23. BASIN	W.	Boat ____; Jamal and Tito liked to visit this place.
L - 24. OSWALDO	X.	Kids were sent to Mr. ____ if they were in trouble.
K - 25. FIVE	Y.	____ Rico; Tito went here after the fight

Scorpions Matching 2

___ 1. JEVON   A. Mack's age
___ 2. PUERTO   B. Mrs. ____ wondered what her family was coming to.
___ 3. BASIN   C. Randy's age
___ 4. BOATS   D. Jamal liked to ____ and paint.
___ 5. SEVENTH   E. Reverend ____; prayed with the family
___ 6. EIGHT   F. Last name of boy who raced down the stairs in school with Jamal
___ 7. HICKS   G. Jerry ____; roughest kid in the school
___ 8. GREEN   H. Jamal pulled the gun on him during a fight.
___ 9. BIGGS   I. Said Jamal didn't have any experience
___10. ANGEL   J. Jamal and Tito dreamed of owning them.
___11. BURN   K. Boat ____; Jamal and Tito liked to visit this place.
___12. SIXTEEN   L. Randy used to be their leader.
___13. DRAW   M. ____Hicks; told Jamal to act more like a young man
___14. SEVENTEEN   N. First name of boy who raced down the stairs in school with Jamal
___15. MARCUS   O. Mrs. Rich said Jamal might spend another year in ____ grade.
___16. SPOFFORD   P. ____ Rico; Tito went here after the fight
___17. BLOOD   Q. ____Garvey; name of the park
___18. CELIA   R. Mama's ailment
___19. SCORPIONS   S. ____ Rodriguez wanted to borrow fifteen cents from Jamal or Tito.
___20. DWAYNE   T. Mr. ____, principal; didn't notice when Jamal was on time
___21. VELASQUEZ   U. ____ Haven; Randy was in prison there
___22. WHALEY   V. Mr. ____ would not loan Mama the money.
___23. STANTON   W. First to notice Jamal's gun
___24. OSWALDO   X. Sassy's age
___25. DAVIDSON   Y. Prison where Mack had been

Scorpions Matching 2 Answer Key

M - 1. JEVON	A.	Mack's age
P - 2. PUERTO	B.	Mrs. ____ wondered what her family was coming to.
K - 3. BASIN	C.	Randy's age
J - 4. BOATS	D.	Jamal liked to ____ and paint.
O - 5. SEVENTH	E.	Reverend ____; prayed with the family
X - 6. EIGHT	F.	Last name of boy who raced down the stairs in school with Jamal
B - 7. HICKS	G.	Jerry ____; roughest kid in the school
U - 8. GREEN	H.	Jamal pulled the gun on him during a fight.
E - 9. BIGGS	I.	Said Jamal didn't have any experience
I - 10. ANGEL	J.	Jamal and Tito dreamed of owning them.
R - 11. BURN	K.	Boat ____; Jamal and Tito liked to visit this place.
A - 12. SIXTEEN	L.	Randy used to be their leader.
D - 13. DRAW	M.	____Hicks; told Jamal to act more like a young man
C - 14. SEVENTEEN	N.	First name of boy who raced down the stairs in school with Jamal
Q - 15. MARCUS	O.	Mrs. Rich said Jamal might spend another year in ____ grade.
Y - 16. SPOFFORD	P.	____ Rico; Tito went here after the fight
W - 17. BLOOD	Q.	____Garvey; name of the park
S - 18. CELIA	R.	Mama's ailment
L - 19. SCORPIONS	S.	____ Rodriguez wanted to borrow fifteen cents from Jamal or Tito.
H - 20. DWAYNE	T.	Mr. ____, principal; didn't notice when Jamal was on time
F - 21. VELASQUEZ	U.	____ Haven; Randy was in prison there
G - 22. WHALEY	V.	Mr. ____ would not loan Mama the money.
V - 23. STANTON	W.	First to notice Jamal's gun
N - 24. OSWALDO	X.	Sassy's age
T - 25. DAVIDSON	Y.	Prison where Mack had been

Scorpions Matching 3

___ 1. BURN   A. ____ Hicks; told Jamal to act more like a young man
___ 2. FOURTEEN   B. Mack's age
___ 3. DRAW   C. ____ Rico; Tito went here after the fight
___ 4. GUN   D. Sassy's age
___ 5. STANTON   E. Jamal liked to ____ and paint.
___ 6. TWO   F. Jamal's older brother who was in jail
___ 7. ASTHMA   G. Randy's age
___ 8. CELIA   H. What Mack gave Jamal
___ 9. DWAYNE   I. The lawyer wanted ____ thousand dollars for the appeal.
___ 10. SEVENTEEN   J. Tito's ailment
___ 11. TITO   K. First name of boy who raced down the stairs in school with Jamal
___ 12. HARLEM   L. ____ Cruz; Jamal's best friend
___ 13. ROBERTS   M. Mr. ____ would not loan Mama the money.
___ 14. PUERTO   N. ____ Garvey; name of the park
___ 15. SIXTEEN   O. Mama's ailment
___ 16. OSWALDO   P. Mrs. ____ gave peppermints to students.
___ 17. RANDY   Q. ____ Haven; Randy was in prison there
___ 18. HICKS   R. Mrs. ____ wondered what her family was coming to.
___ 19. TWELVE   S. ____ Rodriguez wanted to borrow fifteen cents from Jamal or Tito.
___ 20. DAVIDSON   T. Mr. ____, principal; didn't notice when Jamal was on time
___ 21. JEVON   U. Angel's age
___ 22. MARCUS   V. Setting of the novel
___ 23. GREEN   W. Jamal's age
___ 24. DARNELL   X. Jamal pulled the gun on him during a fight.
___ 25. EIGHT   Y. Asked Jamal if he had a gun

Scorpions Matching 3 Answer Key

O - 1. BURN
U - 2. FOURTEEN
E - 3. DRAW
H - 4. GUN
M - 5. STANTON
I - 6. TWO
J - 7. ASTHMA
S - 8. CELIA
X - 9. DWAYNE
G - 10. SEVENTEEN
L - 11. TITO
V - 12. HARLEM
P - 13. ROBERTS
C - 14. PUERTO
B - 15. SIXTEEN
K - 16. OSWALDO
F - 17. RANDY
R - 18. HICKS
W - 19. TWELVE
T - 20. DAVIDSON
A - 21. JEVON
N - 22. MARCUS
Q - 23. GREEN
Y - 24. DARNELL
D - 25. EIGHT

A. ____ Hicks; told Jamal to act more like a young man
B. Mack's age
C. ____ Rico; Tito went here after the fight
D. Sassy's age
E. Jamal liked to ____ and paint.
F. Jamal's older brother who was in jail
G. Randy's age
H. What Mack gave Jamal
I. The lawyer wanted ____ thousand dollars for the appeal.
J. Tito's ailment
K. First name of boy who raced down the stairs in school with Jamal
L. ____ Cruz; Jamal's best friend
M. Mr. ____ would not loan Mama the money.
N. ____ Garvey; name of the park
O. Mama's ailment
P. Mrs. ____ gave peppermints to students.
Q. ____ Haven; Randy was in prison there
R. Mrs. ____ wondered what her family was coming to.
S. ____ Rodriguez wanted to borrow fifteen cents from Jamal or Tito.
T. Mr. ____, principal; didn't notice when Jamal was on time
U. Angel's age
V. Setting of the novel
W. Jamal's age
X. Jamal pulled the gun on him during a fight.
Y. Asked Jamal if he had a gun

Scorpions Matching 4

___ 1. ANGEL   A. Wondered if Jamal 'had the heart'
___ 2. DRAWING   B. Said Jamal didn't have any experience
___ 3. TWELVE   C. Mack's age
___ 4. TWO   D. The lawyer wanted ____ thousand dollars for the appeal.
___ 5. STANTON   E. Jamal's age
___ 6. GREEN   F. Mama's ailment
___ 7. HICKS   G. ____ Rico; Tito went here after the fight
___ 8. BIGGS   H. Turned Randy in to a cop a plea.
___ 9. JEVON   I. Jamal liked to ____ and paint.
___10. BURN   J. Mrs. ____ wondered what her family was coming to.
___11. ASTHMA   K. Mr. ____ would not loan Mama the money.
___12. BLOOD   L. ____Hicks; told Jamal to act more like a young man
___13. SIXTEEN   M. Mrs. ____ asked Jamal if he would ever pay attention in class
___14. HARLEM   N. Didn't like Dwayne; gave him a disgusted look
___15. GONZALEZ   O. Boat ____; Jamal and Tito liked to visit this place.
___16. INDIAN   P. Tito's ailment
___17. ABUELA   Q. Randy used to be their leader.
___18. DRAW   R. Reverend ____; prayed with the family
___19. RICH   S. First to notice Jamal's gun
___20. PUERTO   T. Setting of the novel
___21. SINGH   U. Jamal worked in his bodega.
___22. MYRNA   V. ____ Haven; Randy was in prison there
___23. BASIN   W. Tito's grandmother
___24. SCORPIONS   X. Kids were sent to Mr. ____ if they were in trouble.
___25. WILLIE   Y. Jamal gave one of his to Tito when he left.

Scorpions Matching 4 Answer Key

B - 1. ANGEL	A.	Wondered if Jamal 'had the heart'
Y - 2. DRAWING	B.	Said Jamal didn't have any experience
E - 3. TWELVE	C.	Mack's age
D - 4. TWO	D.	The lawyer wanted ____ thousand dollars for the appeal.
K - 5. STANTON	E.	Jamal's age
V - 6. GREEN	F.	Mama's ailment
J - 7. HICKS	G.	____ Rico; Tito went here after the fight
R - 8. BIGGS	H.	Turned Randy in to a cop a plea.
L - 9. JEVON	I.	Jamal liked to ____ and paint.
F - 10. BURN	J.	Mrs. ____ wondered what her family was coming to.
P - 11. ASTHMA	K.	Mr. ____ would not loan Mama the money.
S - 12. BLOOD	L.	____ Hicks; told Jamal to act more like a young man
C - 13. SIXTEEN	M.	Mrs. ____ asked Jamal if he would ever pay attention in class
T - 14. HARLEM	N.	Didn't like Dwayne; gave him a disgusted look
U - 15. GONZALEZ	O.	Boat ____; Jamal and Tito liked to visit this place.
A - 16. INDIAN	P.	Tito's ailment
W - 17. ABUELA	Q.	Randy used to be their leader.
I - 18. DRAW	R.	Reverend ____; prayed with the family
M - 19. RICH	S.	First to notice Jamal's gun
G - 20. PUERTO	T.	Setting of the novel
X - 21. SINGH	U.	Jamal worked in his bodega.
N - 22. MYRNA	V.	____ Haven; Randy was in prison there
O - 23. BASIN	W.	Tito's grandmother
Q - 24. SCORPIONS	X.	Kids were sent to Mr. ____ if they were in trouble.
H - 25. WILLIE	Y.	Jamal gave one of his to Tito when he left.

Scorpions Magic Squares 1

Match the definition with the vocabulary word. Put your answers in the magic squares below. When your answers are correct, all columns and rows will add to the same number.

A. JEVON   E. VELASQUEZ   I. TITO   M. TWO
B. CATHOLIC   F. ABUELA   J. WHALEY   N. STANTON
C. TWELVE   G. SEVENTH   K. GUN   O. MACK
D. OSWALDO   H. EIGHT   L. BASIN   P. FIREHOUSE

1. ____Hicks; told Jamal to act more like a young man
2. Mr. ____ would not loan Mama the money.
3. Jerry ____; roughest kid in the school
4. Last name of boy who raced down the stairs in school with Jamal
5. Mrs. Rich said Jamal might spend another year in ____ grade.
6. Boat ____; Jamal and Tito liked to visit this place.
7. Scorpion's base was an old one
8. Jamal's age
9. Gave the gun to Jamal
10. First name of boy who raced down the stairs in school with Jamal
11. Sassy's age
12. What Mack gave Jamal
13. ____ Cruz; Jamal's best friend
14. Tito's grandmother
15. Tito's religion
16. The lawyer wanted ____ thousand dollars for the appeal.

A=	B=	C=	D=
E=	F=	G=	H=
I=	J=	K=	L=
M=	N=	O=	P=

Scorpions Magic Squares 1 Answer Key

Match the definition with the vocabulary word. Put your answers in the magic squares below. When your answers are correct, all columns and rows will add to the same number.

A. JEVON
B. CATHOLIC
C. TWELVE
D. OSWALDO
E. VELASQUEZ
F. ABUELA
G. SEVENTH
H. EIGHT
I. TITO
J. WHALEY
K. GUN
L. BASIN
M. TWO
N. STANTON
O. MACK
P. FIREHOUSE

1. ____Hicks; told Jamal to act more like a young man
2. Mr. ____ would not loan Mama the money.
3. Jerry ____; roughest kid in the school
4. Last name of boy who raced down the stairs in school with Jamal
5. Mrs. Rich said Jamal might spend another year in ____ grade.
6. Boat ____; Jamal and Tito liked to visit this place.
7. Scorpion's base was an old one
8. Jamal's age
9. Gave the gun to Jamal
10. First name of boy who raced down the stairs in school with Jamal
11. Sassy's age
12. What Mack gave Jamal
13. ____ Cruz; Jamal's best friend
14. Tito's grandmother
15. Tito's religion
16. The lawyer wanted ____ thousand dollars for the appeal.

A=1	B=15	C=8	D=10
E=4	F=14	G=5	H=11
I=13	J=3	K=12	L=6
M=16	N=2	O=9	P=7

Scorpions Magic Squares 2

Match the definition with the vocabulary word. Put your answers in the magic squares below. When your answers are correct, all columns and rows will add to the same number.

A. BIGGS
B. CELIA
C. ROBERTS
D. ABUELA
E. OSWALDO
F. ASTHMA
G. SEVENTH
H. DAVIDSON
I. DRAW
J. FIREHOUSE
K. HARLEM
L. INDIAN
M. SIXTEEN
N. DARNELL
O. SPOFFORD
P. MARCUS

1. Prison where Mack had been
2. Tito's grandmother
3. Scorpion's base was an old one
4. First name of boy who raced down the stairs in school with Jamal
5. Jamal liked to ____ and paint.
6. Tito's ailment
7. ____ Garvey; name of the park
8. Mrs. ____ gave peppermints to students.
9. Mr. ____, principal; didn't notice when Jamal was on time
10. Setting of the novel
11. Reverend ____; prayed with the family
12. Asked Jamal if he had a gun
13. ____ Rodriguez wanted to borrow fifteen cents from Jamal or Tito.
14. Mack's age
15. Mrs. Rich said Jamal might spend another year in ____ grade.
16. Wondered if Jamal 'had the heart'

A=	B=	C=	D=
E=	F=	G=	H=
I=	J=	K=	L=
M=	N=	O=	P=

Scorpions Magic Squares 2 Answer Key

Match the definition with the vocabulary word. Put your answers in the magic squares below. When your answers are correct, all columns and rows will add to the same number.

A. BIGGS
B. CELIA
C. ROBERTS
D. ABUELA
E. OSWALDO
F. ASTHMA
G. SEVENTH
H. DAVIDSON
I. DRAW
J. FIREHOUSE
K. HARLEM
L. INDIAN
M. SIXTEEN
N. DARNELL
O. SPOFFORD
P. MARCUS

1. Prison where Mack had been
2. Tito's grandmother
3. Scorpion's base was an old one
4. First name of boy who raced down the stairs in school with Jamal
5. Jamal liked to ____ and paint.
6. Tito's ailment
7. ____Garvey; name of the park
8. Mrs. ____ gave peppermints to students.
9. Mr. ____, principal; didn't notice when Jamal was on time
10. Setting of the novel
11. Reverend ____; prayed with the family
12. Asked Jamal if he had a gun
13. ____ Rodriguez wanted to borrow fifteen cents from Jamal or Tito.
14. Mack's age
15. Mrs. Rich said Jamal might spend another year in ____ grade.
16. Wondered if Jamal 'had the heart'

A=11	B=13	C=8	D=2
E=4	F=6	G=15	H=9
I=5	J=3	K=10	L=16
M=14	N=12	O=1	P=7

Scorpions Magic Squares 3

Match the definition with the vocabulary word. Put your answers in the magic squares below. When your answers are correct, all columns and rows will add to the same number.

A. MITCHELL   E. GREEN   I. GONZALEZ   M. ABUELA
B. ASTHMA   F. EIGHT   J. STANTON   N. MACK
C. DARNELL   G. MARCUS   K. SCORPIONS O. CATHOLIC
D. DAVIDSON H. GUN   L. ANGEL   P. FOURTEEN

1. Asked Jamal if he had a gun
2. Mr. ____ would not loan Mama the money.
3. Sassy's age
4. Tito's religion
5. Angel's age
6. ____ Haven; Randy was in prison there
7. Jamal worked in his bodega.
8. Mr. ____, principal; didn't notice when Jamal was on time
9. Tito's grandmother
10. What Mack gave Jamal
11. Said Jamal didn't have any experience
12. Mrs. ____ told Dwayne to stay after school.
13. Tito's ailment
14. Randy used to be their leader.
15. ____ Garvey; name of the park
16. Gave the gun to Jamal

A=	B=	C=	D=
E=	F=	G=	H=
I=	J=	K=	L=
M=	N=	O=	P=

Scorpions Magic Squares 3 Answer Key

Match the definition with the vocabulary word. Put your answers in the magic squares below. When your answers are correct, all columns and rows will add to the same number.

A. MITCHELL   E. GREEN   I. GONZALEZ   M. ABUELA
B. ASTHMA   F. EIGHT   J. STANTON   N. MACK
C. DARNELL   G. MARCUS   K. SCORPIONS   O. CATHOLIC
D. DAVIDSON   H. GUN   L. ANGEL   P. FOURTEEN

1. Asked Jamal if he had a gun
2. Mr. ____ would not loan Mama the money.
3. Sassy's age
4. Tito's religion
5. Angel's age
6. ____ Haven; Randy was in prison there
7. Jamal worked in his bodega.
8. Mr. ____, principal; didn't notice when Jamal was on time
9. Tito's grandmother
10. What Mack gave Jamal
11. Said Jamal didn't have any experience
12. Mrs. ____ told Dwayne to stay after school.
13. Tito's ailment
14. Randy used to be their leader.
15. ____Garvey; name of the park
16. Gave the gun to Jamal

A=12	B=13	C=1	D=8
E=6	F=3	G=15	H=10
I=7	J=2	K=14	L=11
M=9	N=16	O=4	P=5

Scorpions Magic Squares 4

Match the definition with the vocabulary word. Put your answers in the magic squares below. When your answers are correct, all columns and rows will add to the same number.

A. SPOFFORD   E. PUERTO   I. ROBERTS   M. SEVENTEEN
B. MACK   F. SCORPIONS J. DAVIDSON   N. CELIA
C. JEVON   G. GREEN   K. ANGEL   O. HICKS
D. SINGH   H. WHALEY   L. BIGGS   P. STANTON

1. Gave the gun to Jamal
2. ____ Haven; Randy was in prison there
3. Said Jamal didn't have any experience
4. ____ Rodriguez wanted to borrow fifteen cents from Jamal or Tito.
5. Randy's age
6. Reverend ____; prayed with the family
7. Jerry ____; roughest kid in the school
8. Prison where Mack had been
9. Mr. ____ would not loan Mama the money.
10. Mrs. ____ gave peppermints to students.
11. ____ Rico; Tito went here after the fight
12. Kids were sent to Mr. ____ if they were in trouble.
13. ____ Hicks; told Jamal to act more like a young man
14. Randy used to be their leader.
15. Mr. ____, principal; didn't notice when Jamal was on time
16. Mrs. ____ wondered what her family was coming to.

A=	B=	C=	D=
E=	F=	G=	H=
I=	J=	K=	L=
M=	N=	O=	P=

Scorpions Magic Squares 4 Answer Key

Match the definition with the vocabulary word. Put your answers in the magic squares below. When your answers are correct, all columns and rows will add to the same number.

A. SPOFFORD   E. PUERTO   I. ROBERTS   M. SEVENTEEN
B. MACK   F. SCORPIONS   J. DAVIDSON   N. CELIA
C. JEVON   G. GREEN   K. ANGEL   O. HICKS
D. SINGH   H. WHALEY   L. BIGGS   P. STANTON

1. Gave the gun to Jamal
2. ____ Haven; Randy was in prison there
3. Said Jamal didn't have any experience
4. ____ Rodriguez wanted to borrow fifteen cents from Jamal or Tito.
5. Randy's age
6. Reverend ____; prayed with the family
7. Jerry ____; roughest kid in the school
8. Prison where Mack had been
9. Mr. ____ would not loan Mama the money.
10. Mrs. ____ gave peppermints to students.
11. ____ Rico; Tito went here after the fight
12. Kids were sent to Mr. ____ if they were in trouble.
13. ____ Hicks; told Jamal to act more like a young man
14. Randy used to be their leader.
15. Mr. ____, principal; didn't notice when Jamal was on time
16. Mrs. ____ wondered what her family was coming to.

A=8	B=1	C=13	D=12
E=11	F=14	G=2	H=7
I=10	J=15	K=3	L=6
M=5	N=4	O=16	P=9

Scorpions Word Search 1

```
M S E V E N T E E N A N G E L B C A Y
I W I D R A W I N G R F V T J E P D R
T M N V F R C I F F P I E M L I H D G
C M D B D P O S L R V V L I M G Y I R
H B I G G S X B I L K E A A K H E S Y
E L A H I N S D E X I Y S B S T L O L
L C N N E H R X C R T E Q T R T A N M
L Q G E Y O T F S K T E U J R O H D T
H H R S F I R E H O U S E D R A W M Q
I G T F T H O T N T B V Z N B A X N A
C T O F H D N G D Q O D Y M Y L P T M
K P R W L E Q R N N L W T N V D O W N
S B J A V P U E R T O M E L R A H O D
P P W E N C J N H M K E A X W R B T D
X S S C V D I M D A T C Y C W N U W H
O B O A T S Y V N R I C H O K E R E Q
X M V Q A R X U U C P G T K G L N L D
D J R B N L G O M U M I Z W K L J V F
R H S A K S F V Y S T G O N Z A L E Z
```

Angel's age (8)
Asked Jamal if he had a gun (7)
At first the lawyer wanted ____ hundred dollars for the appeal. (4)
Boat ____; Jamal and Tito liked to visit this place. (5)
Didn't like Dwayne; gave him a disgusted look (5)
First name of boy who raced down the stairs in school with Jamal (7)
First to notice Jamal's gun (5)
Gave the gun to Jamal (4)
Jamal and Tito dreamed of owning them. (5)
Jamal gave one of his to Tito when he left. (7)
Jamal liked to ____ and paint. (4)
Jamal pulled the gun on him during a fight. (6)
Jamal worked in his bodega. (8)
Jamal's age (6)
Jamal's older brother who was in jail (5)
Jerry ____; roughest kid in the school (6)
Kids were sent to Mr. ____ if they were in trouble. (5)
Last name of boy who raced down the stairs in school with Jamal (9)
Mack's age (7)
Mama's ailment (4)
Miss ____; Jamal's favorite teacher (5)
Mr. ____ was Randy's lawyer. (7)
Mrs. Rich said Jamal might spend another year in ____ grade. (7)

Mrs. ____ gave peppermints to students. (7)
Mrs. ____ told Dwayne to stay after school. (8)
Mrs. ____ wondered what her family was coming to. (5)
Mrs. ____ asked Jamal if he would ever pay attention in class (4)
Prison where Mack had been (8)
Randy's age (9)
Reverend ____; prayed with the family (5)
Said Jamal didn't have any experience (5)
Sassy's age (5)
Scorpion's base was an old one (9)
Setting of the novel (6)
The lawyer wanted ____ thousand dollars for the appeal. (3)
Tito's ailment (6)
Turned Randy in to a cop a plea. (6)
What Mack gave Jamal (3)
Wondered if Jamal 'had the heart' (6)
____ Cruz; Jamal's best friend (4)
____ Haven; Randy was in prison there (5)
____ Rico; Tito went here after the fight (6)
____ Rodriguez wanted to borrow fifteen cents from Jamal or Tito. (5)
____ Garvey; name of the park (6)
____ Hicks; told Jamal to act more like a young man (5)

Scorpions Word Search 1 Answer Key

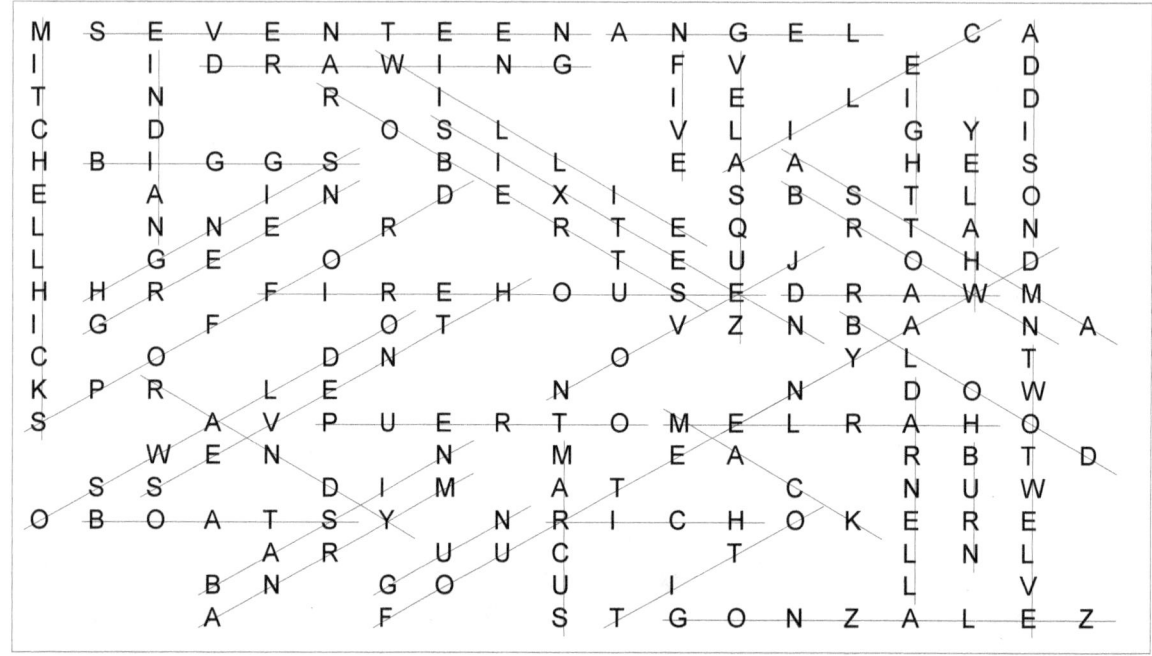

Angel's age (8)
Asked Jamal if he had a gun (7)
At first the lawyer wanted ____ hundred dollars for the appeal. (4)
Boat ____; Jamal and Tito liked to visit this place. (5)
Didn't like Dwayne; gave him a disgusted look (5)
First name of boy who raced down the stairs in school with Jamal (7)
First to notice Jamal's gun (5)
Gave the gun to Jamal (4)
Jamal and Tito dreamed of owning them. (5)
Jamal gave one of his to Tito when he left. (7)
Jamal liked to ____ and paint. (4)
Jamal pulled the gun on him during a fight. (6)
Jamal worked in his bodega. (8)
Jamal's age (6)
Jamal's older brother who was in jail (5)
Jerry ____; roughest kid in the school (6)
Kids were sent to Mr. ____ if they were in trouble. (5)
Last name of boy who raced down the stairs in school with Jamal (9)
Mack's age (7)
Mama's ailment (4)
Miss ____; Jamal's favorite teacher (5)
Mr. ____ was Randy's lawyer. (7)
Mrs. Rich said Jamal might spend another year in ____ grade. (7)

Mrs. ____ gave peppermints to students. (7)
Mrs. ____ told Dwayne to stay after school. (8)
Mrs. ____ wondered what her family was coming to. (5)
Mrs. ____ asked Jamal if he would ever pay attention in class (4)
Prison where Mack had been (8)
Randy's age (9)
Reverend ____; prayed with the family (5)
Said Jamal didn't have any experience (5)
Sassy's age (5)
Scorpion's base was an old one (9)
Setting of the novel (6)
The lawyer wanted ____ thousand dollars for the appeal. (3)
Tito's ailment (6)
Turned Randy in to a cop a plea. (6)
What Mack gave Jamal (3)
Wondered if Jamal 'had the heart' (6)
____ Cruz; Jamal's best friend (4)
____ Haven; Randy was in prison there (5)
____ Rico; Tito went here after the fight (6)
____ Rodriguez wanted to borrow fifteen cents from Jamal or Tito. (5)
____ Garvey; name of the park (6)
____ Hicks; told Jamal to act more like a young man (5)

Scorpions Word Search 2

```
M N T A B O A T S B H A R L E M T N H
Y A V F N G X Q W Y I P D I K K I W L
R M C C H G O Y D O C S R R N S T O J
N K S K P C E N J C K I A Q A D O R N
A T T N M D A L Z S S X W B A R I B L
L B A G Y R H R A A W T I R Z O Q A D
J J N B I G G S S R L E N L H F X N N
J W T L L E H C T I M E G J W F H F O
O H O V J T Q Y H Z L N Z G I O Z R S
X S N D N G X Y M L L L H B L P J M D
S T W E L V E F A Q B V F T L S Q W I
F E V A K C O B C J G U H G I O A A V
M E V T L U W Q J Q B G R J E R O D A
S A Q E R D W W T R I Z O N D T L D D
S B M T N C O H G E G J B J F S G I P
Z U E Q L T E A P R R E E P I R M S N
S E T V V Y E L E V I V R F V Z N O V
N L D W A Y N E I F C O T R E U P N X
M A R C U S N Y N A H N S H G N I S L
```

Angel's age (8)
Asked Jamal if he had a gun (7)
At first the lawyer wanted ____ hundred dollars for the appeal. (4)
Boat ____; Jamal and Tito liked to visit this place. (5)
Didn't like Dwayne; gave him a disgusted look (5)
First name of boy who raced down the stairs in school with Jamal (7)
First to notice Jamal's gun (5)
Gave the gun to Jamal (4)
Jamal and Tito dreamed of owning them. (5)
Jamal gave one of his to Tito when he left. (7)
Jamal liked to ____ and paint. (4)
Jamal pulled the gun on him during a fight. (6)
Jamal worked in his bodega. (8)
Jamal's age (6)
Jamal's older brother who was in jail (5)
Jerry ____; roughest kid in the school (6)
Kids were sent to Mr. ____ if they were in trouble. (5)
Mack's age (7)
Mama's ailment (4)
Miss ____; Jamal's favorite teacher (5)
Mr. ____ was Randy's lawyer. (7)
Mr. ____ would not loan Mama the money. (7)
Mr. ____, principal; didn't notice when Jamal was on time (8)
Mrs. Rich said Jamal might spend another year in ____ grade. (7)
Mrs. ____ gave peppermints to students. (7)
Mrs. ____ told Dwayne to stay after school. (8)
Mrs. ____ wondered what her family was coming to. (5)
Mrs. ____ asked Jamal if he would ever pay attention in class (4)
Prison where Mack had been (8)
Randy's age (9)
Reverend ____; prayed with the family (5)
Said Jamal didn't have any experience (5)
Sassy's age (5)
Setting of the novel (6)
The lawyer wanted ____ thousand dollars for the appeal. (3)
Tito's ailment (6)
Tito's grandmother (6)
Turned Randy in to a cop a plea. (6)
What Mack gave Jamal (3)
Wondered if Jamal 'had the heart' (6)
____ Cruz; Jamal's best friend (4)
____ Haven; Randy was in prison there (5)
____ Rico; Tito went here after the fight (6)
____ Rodriguez wanted to borrow fifteen cents from Jamal or Tito. (5)
____ Garvey; name of the park (6)
____ Hicks; told Jamal to act more like a young man (5)

Scorpions Word Search 2 Answer Key

```
M        A  B  O  A  T  S     H  A  R  L  E  M  T  N
Y  A        N  G        W  I     D  I        I  W
R  C           G  O     D  O  C  S  R     N  S  T  O
N  S  K        E  N        K  I  A     A  D  O  R  B
A  T        A  L  Z     A  S  X  W  B  A  R  I  B  A
   A     R        A     S  T     R     O     O     
   N  B  I  G  G  S  S     L  E  N     F        N  
   T  L  L  E  H  C  T  I  M  E  G  W  F        O  
O     O     T        H     L  N     I  O        S  
   S  N     N        M  L     B     L  P        D  
S  T  W  E  L  V  E  F  A     B     T  L  S     W  I
   E  V  A        O        U  H     I  O  A     V  
   E  V        L  U        G  R     E  R  O  D  A  
S  A     E  R  D     W        O  N  D     D  D  A  D
   B     T  N  C  O  H     E  G  J  B     F  I     
   U  E        T  E  A     R  R  E  E     I  S     
   E           E  L  E     I  V  R     V  N  O     
N  L  D  W  A  Y  N  E  I  C  O  T  R  E  U  P  N  
M  A  R  C  U  S  N  Y  N  A  H  N  S  H  G  N  I  S
```

Angel's age (8)
Asked Jamal if he had a gun (7)
At first the lawyer wanted ____hundred dollars for the appeal. (4)
Boat ____; Jamal and Tito liked to visit this place. (5)
Didn't like Dwayne; gave him a disgusted look (5)
First name of boy who raced down the stairs in school with Jamal (7)
First to notice Jamal's gun (5)
Gave the gun to Jamal (4)
Jamal and Tito dreamed of owning them. (5)
Jamal gave one of his to Tito when he left. (7)
Jamal liked to ____ and paint. (4)
Jamal pulled the gun on him during a fight. (6)
Jamal worked in his bodega. (8)
Jamal's age (6)
Jamal's older brother who was in jail (5)
Jerry ____; roughest kid in the school (6)
Kids were sent to Mr. ____ if they were in trouble. (5)
Mack's age (7)
Mama's ailment (4)
Miss ____; Jamal's favorite teacher (5)
Mr. ____ was Randy's lawyer. (7)
Mr. ____ would not loan Mama the money. (7)
Mr. ____, principal; didn't notice when Jamal was on time (8)
Mrs. Rich said Jamal might spend another year in ____ grade. (7)
Mrs. ____ gave peppermints to students. (7)
Mrs. ____ told Dwayne to stay after school. (8)
Mrs. ____ wondered what her family was coming to. (5)
Mrs. ____asked Jamal if he would ever pay attention in class (4)
Prison where Mack had been (8)
Randy's age (9)
Reverend ____; prayed with the family (5)
Said Jamal didn't have any experience (5)
Sassy's age (5)
Setting of the novel (6)
The lawyer wanted ____ thousand dollars for the appeal. (3)
Tito's ailment (6)
Tito's grandmother (6)
Turned Randy in to a cop a plea. (6)
What Mack gave Jamal (3)
Wondered if Jamal 'had the heart' (6)
____ Cruz; Jamal's best friend (4)
____ Haven; Randy was in prison there (5)
____ Rico; Tito went here after the fight (6)
____ Rodriguez wanted to borrow fifteen cents from Jamal or Tito. (5)
____Garvey; name of the park (6)
____Hicks; told Jamal to act more like a young man (5)

Scorpions Word Search 3

```
L J Q D R O F F O P S I N D I A N N W
J B Y A G S I X T E E N N W B H B X Y
K Q W V O L C H Z C X T R A S D H G F
Z F D I N B F J B V A F I Y K R D O M
Y X A D Z C B Y H Z G T C N H A S N Q
N T R S A J M Y S I N G H E K W W F S
B H N O L E N L A J J T G O A Y C R R
V R E N E V P H B L W I V L L T D S M
Q E L L Z O T U R R T D B D I W C F
F H L E G N A F E B O O B U R N C O Y
V I W A E W J Y L R X W B T E C M R X
S C S V S T I G A J T S N E R P N P X
B K E N D Q S L V B M O T V R P Z I D
C S M A R C U S L V O N V S M T Z O D
P D Z A X M T E G I E A V P Y P S N D
R G N I W A R D Z V E T T F R G G S S
M D T P N F N C E T H W T S N H C F L
Y S B T G I Y S B G R E E N A A G O X
N V O L S V M L I C J L D K M R W U N
V N Z A O E Q E G P J V Z H A L H R N
D C B X Q O Y R G P D E T I P E A T G
M A C K A D D I S O N S L V F M L E G
M I T C H E L L L D C A E N G G W E L
F I R E H O U S E B C F B R M N Y N V
```

ABUELA	CATHOLIC	FOURTEEN	MITCHELL	SINGH
ADDISON	CELIA	GONZALEZ	MYRNA	SIXTEEN
ANGEL	DARNELL	GREEN	OSWALDO	SPOFFORD
ASTHMA	DAVIDSON	GUN	PUERTO	STANTON
BASIN	DRAW	HARLEM	RANDY	TITO
BIGGS	DRAWING	HICKS	RICH	TWELVE
BLOOD	DWAYNE	INDIAN	ROBERTS	TWO
BOATS	EIGHT	JEVON	SCORPIONS	VELASQUEZ
BROWN	FIREHOUSE	MACK	SEVENTEEN	WHALEY
BURN	FIVE	MARCUS	SEVENTH	WILLIE

Scorpions Word Search 3 Answer Key

ABUELA	CATHOLIC	FOURTEEN	MITCHELL	SINGH
ADDISON	CELIA	GONZALEZ	MYRNA	SIXTEEN
ANGEL	DARNELL	GREEN	OSWALDO	SPOFFORD
ASTHMA	DAVIDSON	GUN	PUERTO	STANTON
BASIN	DRAW	HARLEM	RANDY	TITO
BIGGS	DRAWING	HICKS	RICH	TWELVE
BLOOD	DWAYNE	INDIAN	ROBERTS	TWO
BOATS	EIGHT	JEVON	SCORPIONS	VELASQUEZ
BROWN	FIREHOUSE	MACK	SEVENTEEN	WHALEY
BURN	FIVE	MARCUS	SEVENTH	WILLIE

Scorpions Word Search 4

```
S C V G Q N W O R B R Y A H B L T Z N
E A E O W K I Q T A O Y S Y S O Z C V
V T L N V H L F F S B F T Z N H A W M
E H A Z Q Z L I S I E W H A T D G T W
N O S A T Y I R N N R D M J N D S D S
T L Q L V I E E O T T W A N V G B X F
E I U E N P T H I N S Q Y V M I E R D
E C E Z C H M O P S B X G W I N N L Y
N P Z F M F O U R T E E N H T D D R P
H B M J W A S S O X L Y I A C I S Z K
I V N W B C R E C C Q G W L H A C O C
C P K T V B W C S Q R B A E E N F Q N
K L W H F C F O U D Y G R Y L L G N B
S B B R S S Z S F S P D D C L M P C V
D H J X H S T W H S U V K J F N J S Q
B G A N L A R A M X E Q P E R M Z I F
S Q S R H I Y L N K R V D V M I F N P
V X V G L L L D T T T R E O N A C G T
D W A Y N E D O T W O R A N D Y C H L
B M D R N C M H A F E N B O T K V K S
I H U R U H G R F F R L O V Q H Q M B
G B A N G I D O M Y I L V A B U E L A
G D G L E X P Q M S B V R E B M N F B
S A D D I S O N S I X T E E N E E R G
```

ABUELA	CATHOLIC	FOURTEEN	MITCHELL	SINGH
ADDISON	CELIA	GONZALEZ	MYRNA	SIXTEEN
ANGEL	DARNELL	GREEN	OSWALDO	SPOFFORD
ASTHMA	DAVIDSON	GUN	PUERTO	STANTON
BASIN	DRAW	HARLEM	RANDY	TITO
BIGGS	DRAWING	HICKS	RICH	TWELVE
BLOOD	DWAYNE	INDIAN	ROBERTS	TWO
BOATS	EIGHT	JEVON	SCORPIONS	VELASQUEZ
BROWN	FIREHOUSE	MACK	SEVENTEEN	WHALEY
BURN	FIVE	MARCUS	SEVENTH	WILLIE

Scorpions Word Search 4 Answer Key

ABUELA	CATHOLIC	FOURTEEN	MITCHELL	SINGH
ADDISON	CELIA	GONZALEZ	MYRNA	SIXTEEN
ANGEL	DARNELL	GREEN	OSWALDO	SPOFFORD
ASTHMA	DAVIDSON	GUN	PUERTO	STANTON
BASIN	DRAW	HARLEM	RANDY	TITO
BIGGS	DRAWING	HICKS	RICH	TWELVE
BLOOD	DWAYNE	INDIAN	ROBERTS	TWO
BOATS	EIGHT	JEVON	SCORPIONS	VELASQUEZ
BROWN	FIREHOUSE	MACK	SEVENTEEN	WHALEY
BURN	FIVE	MARCUS	SEVENTH	WILLIE

Scorpions Word Search 1

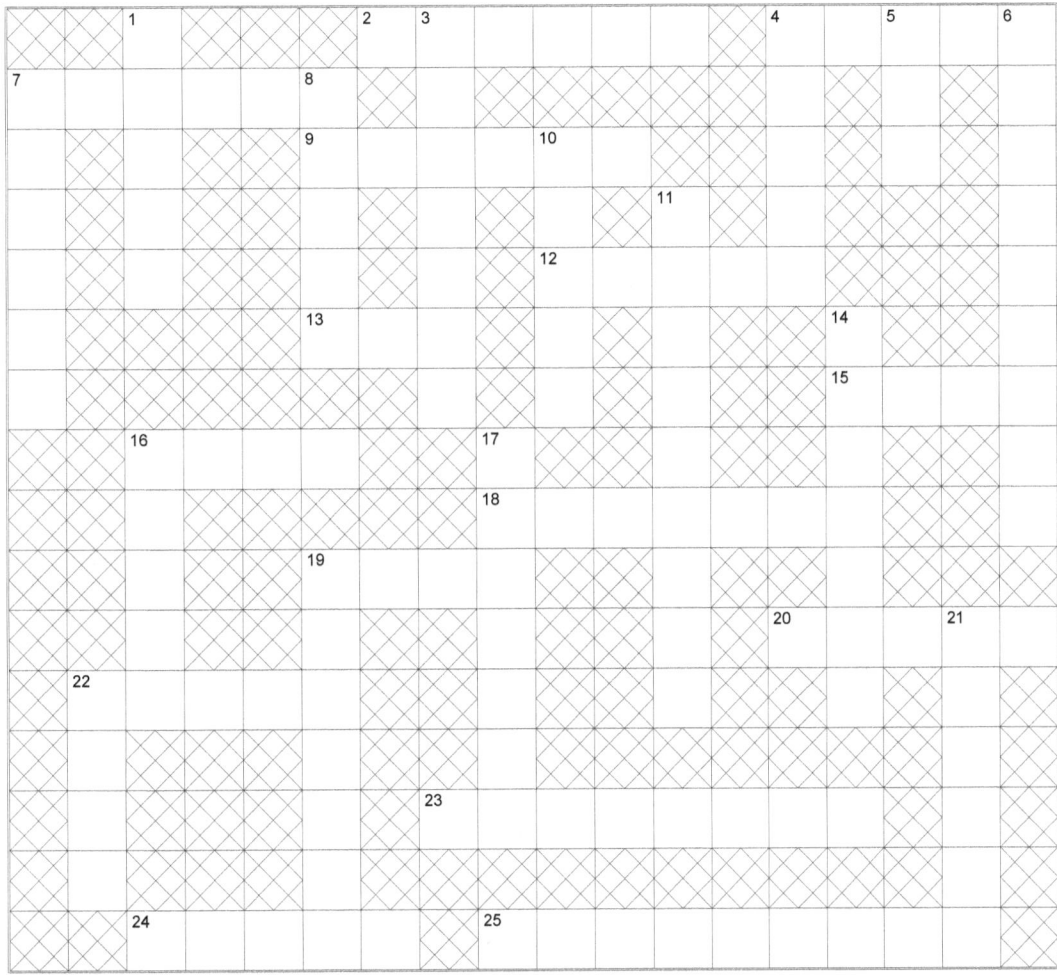

Across
2. Setting of the novel
4. Reverend ____; prayed with the family
7. Turned Randy in to a cop a plea.
9. Wondered if Jamal 'had the heart'
12. ____ Haven; Randy was in prison there
13. The lawyer wanted ____ thousand dollars for the appeal.
15. ____ Cruz; Jamal's best friend
16. Mrs. ____ asked Jamal if he would ever pay attention in class
18. Mack's age
19. Jamal liked to ____ and paint.
20. Jamal and Tito dreamed of owning them.
22. Didn't like Dwayne; gave him a disgusted look
23. Angel's age
24. Kids were sent to Mr. ____ if they were in trouble.
25. Scorpion's base was an old one

Down
1. First to notice Jamal's gun
3. Mr. ____ was Randy's lawyer.
4. Miss ____; Jamal's favorite teacher
5. What Mack gave Jamal
6. Randy used to be their leader.
7. Jerry ____; roughest kid in the school
8. Sassy's age
10. Said Jamal didn't have any experience
11. Randy's age
14. Mr. ____ would not loan Mama the money.
16. Jamal's older brother who was in jail
17. First name of boy who raced down the stairs in school with Jamal
19. Jamal gave one of his to Tito when he left.
21. Jamal's age
22. Gave the gun to Jamal

Scorpions Word Search 1 Answer Key

	1 B		2 H	3 A	R	L	E	M		4 B	I	5 G	G	6 S
7 W	I	L	L	I	8 E		D				R		U		C
H			O		9 N	D	I	A	10 N			O		N	O
A			O			G		I		N	11 S		W			R
L			D			H		S		12 G	R	E	E	N		P
E					13 T	W	O			E	V			14 S		I
Y							N			L	E		15 T	I	T	O
			16 R	I	C	H		17 O			N			A		N
			A					18 S	I	X	T	E	E	N		S
			N		19 D	R	A	W			E		20 B	O	21 A	T	S
		22 M	Y	R	N	A		L			N		N		W
			A			W		D						E
			C			I		23 F	O	U	R	T	E	E	N	L
			K			N									V
			24 S	I	N	G	H		25 F	I	R	E	H	O	U	S	E

Across
2. Setting of the novel
4. Reverend ____; prayed with the family
7. Turned Randy in to a cop a plea.
9. Wondered if Jamal 'had the heart'
12. ____ Haven; Randy was in prison there
13. The lawyer wanted ____ thousand dollars for the appeal.
15. ____ Cruz; Jamal's best friend
16. Mrs. ____ asked Jamal if he would ever pay attention in class
18. Mack's age
19. Jamal liked to ____ and paint.
20. Jamal and Tito dreamed of owning them.
22. Didn't like Dwayne; gave him a disgusted look
23. Angel's age
24. Kids were sent to Mr. ____ if they were in trouble.
25. Scorpion's base was an old one

Down
1. First to notice Jamal's gun
3. Mr. ____ was Randy's lawyer.
4. Miss ____; Jamal's favorite teacher
5. What Mack gave Jamal
6. Randy used to be their leader.
7. Jerry ____; roughest kid in the school
8. Sassy's age
10. Said Jamal didn't have any experience
11. Randy's age
14. Mr. ____ would not loan Mama the money.
16. Jamal's older brother who was in jail
17. First name of boy who raced down the stairs in school with Jamal
19. Jamal gave one of his to Tito when he left.
21. Jamal's age
22. Gave the gun to Jamal

Scorpions Word Search 2

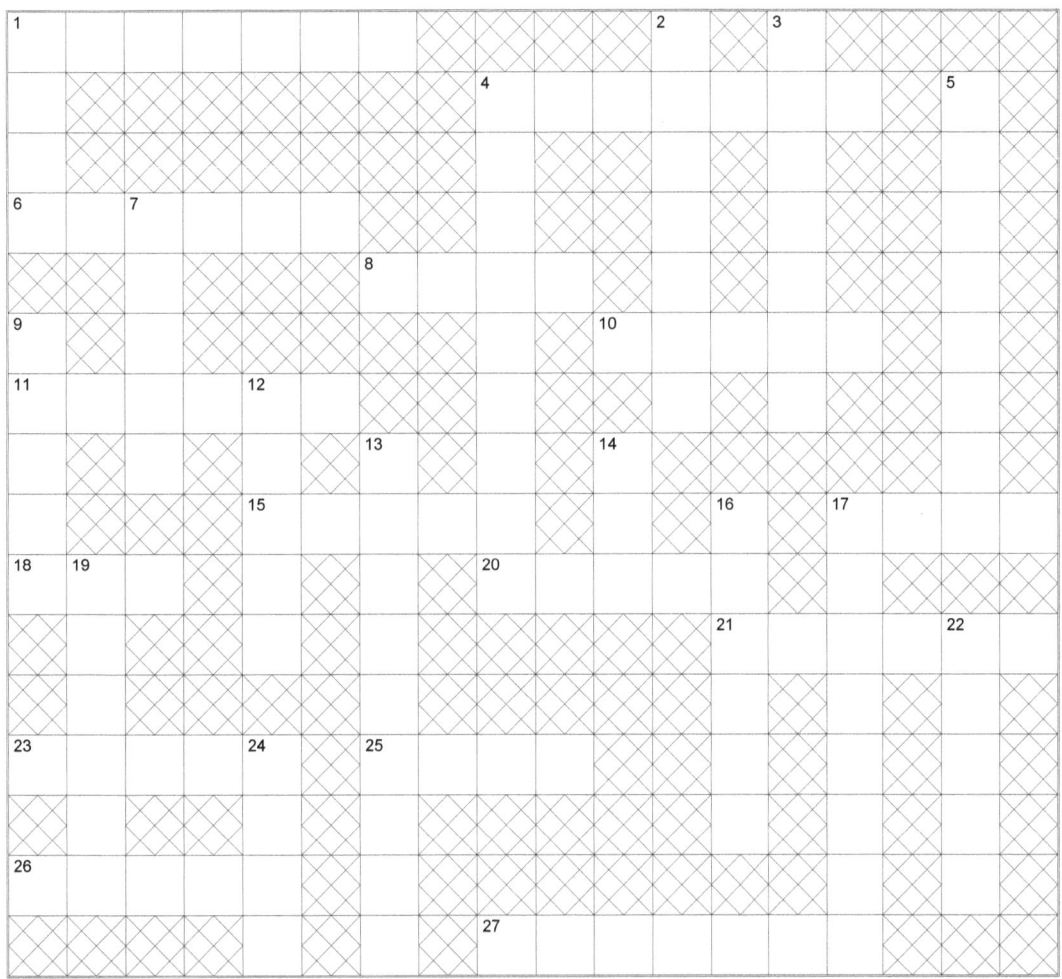

Across
1. Mrs. ____ gave peppermints to students.
4. Mack's age
6. Setting of the novel
8. Mama's ailment
10. Jamal and Tito dreamed of owning them.
11. Wondered if Jamal 'had the heart'
15. ____ Haven; Randy was in prison there
17. Gave the gun to Jamal
18. The lawyer wanted ____ thousand dollars for the appeal.
20. Kids were sent to Mr. ____ if they were in trouble.
21. Tito's ailment
23. First to notice Jamal's gun
25. ____ Cruz; Jamal's best friend
26. ____ Rodriguez wanted to borrow fifteen cents from Jamal or Tito.
27. Asked Jamal if he had a gun

Down
1. Mrs. ____ asked Jamal if he would ever pay attention in class
2. Mr. ____ would not loan Mama the money.
3. Mrs. Rich said Jamal might spend another year in ____ grade.
4. Randy used to be their leader.
5. Tito's religion
7. Jamal's older brother who was in jail
9. Sassy's age
12. Said Jamal didn't have any experience
13. Randy's age
14. What Mack gave Jamal
16. Jerry ____; roughest kid in the school
17. Mrs. ____ told Dwayne to stay after school.
19. Turned Randy in to a cop a plea.
22. Didn't like Dwayne; gave him a disgusted look
24. Jamal liked to ____ and paint.

Scorpions Word Search 2 Answer Key

	1 R	O	B	E	R	T	S			2 S		3 S		
	I					4 S	I	X	T	E	E	N	5 C	
	C					C			A		V		A	
6 H	A	7 R	L	E	M		O		N		E		T	
		A			8 B	U	R	N		T		N		H
9 E		N					P		10 B	O	A	T	S	O
11 I	N	D	I	12 A	N		I		N		H			L
G		Y		N		13 S	O		14 G					I
H			15 G	R	E	E	N		U		16 W		17 M	A	C	K
18 T	19 W	O		E	V		20 S	I	N	G	H		I	
	I			L		E					21 A	S	T	H	22 M	A
	L					N					L		C		Y
23 B	L	O	O	24 D		25 T	I	T	O		E		H		R
	I			R		E					Y		E		N
26 C	E	L	I	A		E		27 D	A	R	N	E	L	L

Across
1. Mrs. ____ gave peppermints to students.
4. Mack's age
6. Setting of the novel
8. Mama's ailment
10. Jamal and Tito dreamed of owning them.
11. Wondered if Jamal 'had the heart'
15. ____ Haven; Randy was in prison there
17. Gave the gun to Jamal
18. The lawyer wanted ____ thousand dollars for the appeal.
20. Kids were sent to Mr. ____ if they were in trouble.
21. Tito's ailment
23. First to notice Jamal's gun
25. ____ Cruz; Jamal's best friend
26. ____ Rodriguez wanted to borrow fifteen cents from Jamal or Tito.
27. Asked Jamal if he had a gun

Down
1. Mrs. ____ asked Jamal if he would ever pay attention in class
2. Mr. ____ would not loan Mama the money.
3. Mrs. Rich said Jamal might spend another year in ____ grade.
4. Randy used to be their leader.
5. Tito's religion
7. Jamal's older brother who was in jail
9. Sassy's age
12. Said Jamal didn't have any experience
13. Randy's age
14. What Mack gave Jamal
16. Jerry ____; roughest kid in the school
17. Mrs. ____ told Dwayne to stay after school.
19. Turned Randy in to a cop a plea.
22. Didn't like Dwayne; gave him a disgusted look
24. Jamal liked to ____ and paint.

Scorpions Word Search 3

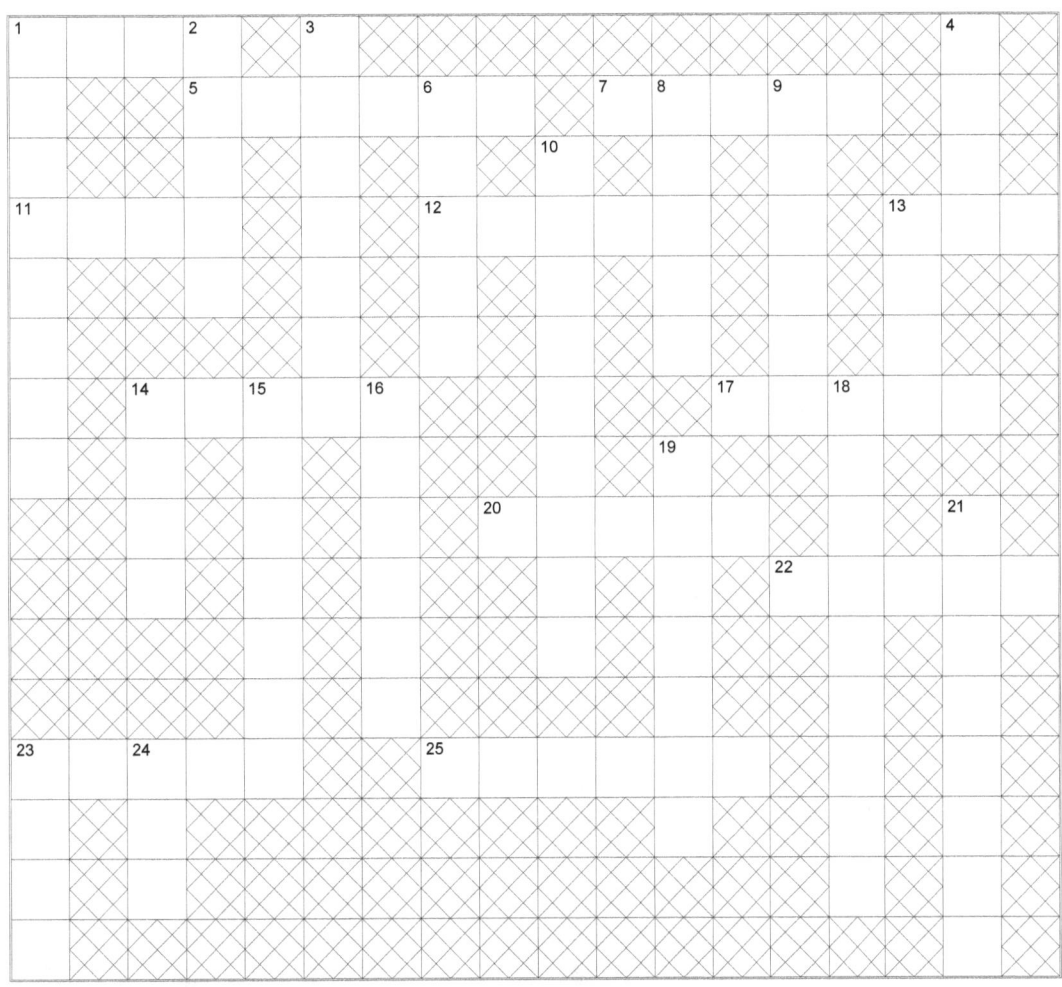

Across
1. At first the lawyer wanted ____ hundred dollars for the appeal.
5. Wondered if Jamal 'had the heart'
7. Miss ____; Jamal's favorite teacher
11. Mrs. ____ asked Jamal if he would ever pay attention in class
12. ____ Haven; Randy was in prison there
13. The lawyer wanted ____ thousand dollars for the appeal.
14. Didn't like Dwayne; gave him a disgusted look
17. ____ Hicks; told Jamal to act more like a young man
20. ____ Rodriguez wanted to borrow fifteen cents from Jamal or Tito.
22. Boat ____; Jamal and Tito liked to visit this place.
23. Reverend ____; prayed with the family
25. Setting of the novel

Down
1. Angel's age
2. Sassy's age
3. Mr. ____ was Randy's lawyer.
4. Jamal liked to ____ and paint.
6. Said Jamal didn't have any experience
8. Jamal's older brother who was in jail
9. Turned Randy in to a cop a plea.
10. Randy's age
13. ____ Cruz; Jamal's best friend
14. Gave the gun to Jamal
15. Mrs. ____ gave peppermints to students.
16. Tito's ailment
18. Last name of boy who raced down the stairs in school with Jamal
19. Mack's age
21. Mrs. ____ told Dwayne to stay after school.
23. Mama's ailment
24. What Mack gave Jamal

Scorpions Word Search 3 Answer Key

	1 F	I	2 V E	A	3 A									4 D	
	O		5 I	N	D	I	6 A	N		7 B	8 R	O	9 W	N	R
	U		G		D		N		10 S		A		I		A
	11 R	I	C	H	I		12 G	R	E	E	N		13 T	W	O
	T		T		S		E		V		D		L		I	
	E				O		L		E		Y		I		T	
	E		14 M	15 Y	R	16 N	A		N			17 J	18 E	V	O	N
	N		A		O		S		T		19 S		E			
			C		B		T		20 C	E	L	I	A		21 M	
			K		E		H		E		I		22 B	A	S	I	N
					R		M		N		T		S		T	
					T		A				E		Q		C	
	23 B	24 I	G	G	S		25 H	A	R	L	E	M	U		H	
	U		U								N		E		E	
	R		N								Z		L		
	N														L	

Across

1. At first the lawyer wanted ____ hundred dollars for the appeal.
5. Wondered if Jamal 'had the heart'
7. Miss ____; Jamal's favorite teacher
11. Mrs. ____ asked Jamal if he would ever pay attention in class
12. ____ Haven; Randy was in prison there
13. The lawyer wanted ____ thousand dollars for the appeal.
14. Didn't like Dwayne; gave him a disgusted look
17. ____ Hicks; told Jamal to act more like a young man
20. ____ Rodriguez wanted to borrow fifteen cents from Jamal or Tito.
22. Boat ____; Jamal and Tito liked to visit this place.
23. Reverend ____; prayed with the family
25. Setting of the novel

Down

1. Angel's age
2. Sassy's age
3. Mr. ____ was Randy's lawyer.
4. Jamal liked to ____ and paint.
6. Said Jamal didn't have any experience
8. Jamal's older brother who was in jail
9. Turned Randy in to a cop a plea.
10. Randy's age
13. ____ Cruz; Jamal's best friend
14. Gave the gun to Jamal
15. Mrs. ____ gave peppermints to students.
16. Tito's ailment
18. Last name of boy who raced down the stairs in school with Jamal
19. Mack's age
21. Mrs. ____ told Dwayne to stay after school.
23. Mama's ailment
24. What Mack gave Jamal

Scorpions Word Search 4

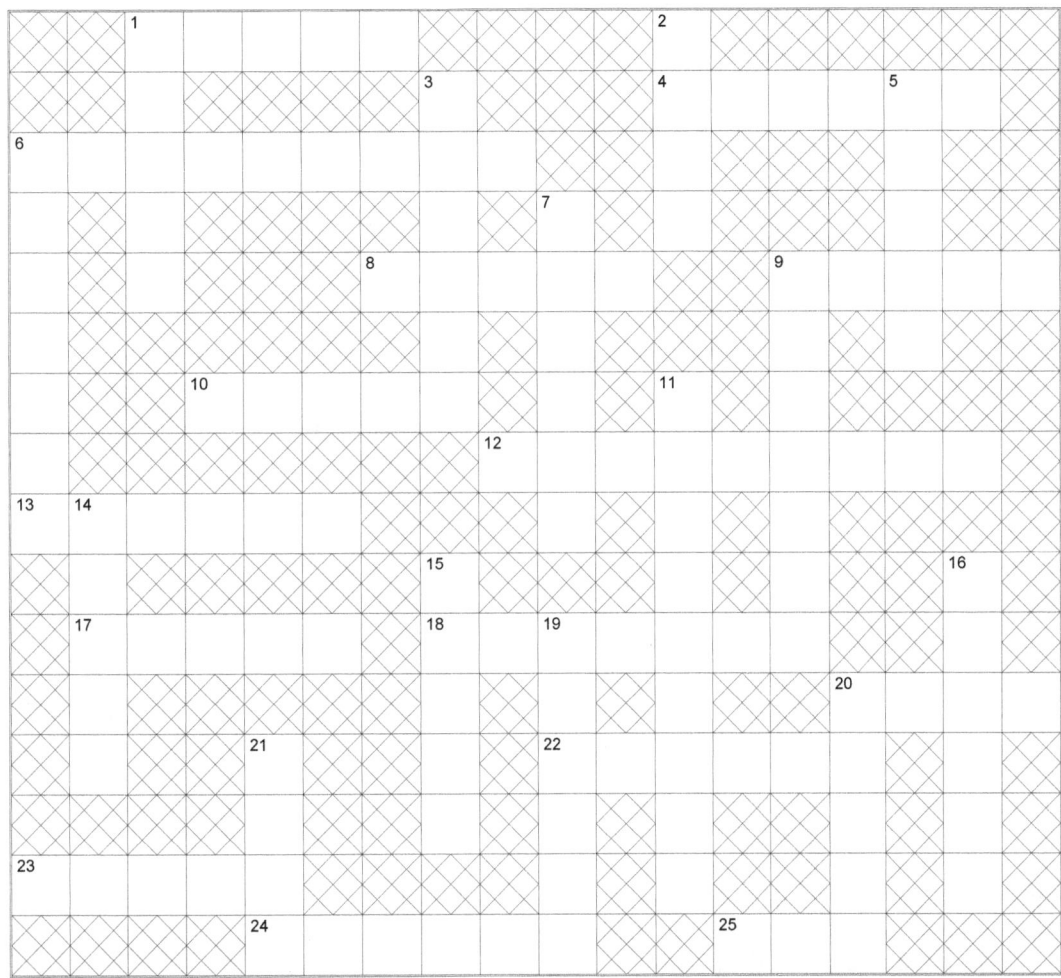

Across
1. First to notice Jamal's gun
4. Tito's ailment
6. Randy used to be their leader.
8. Sassy's age
9. Kids were sent to Mr. ____ if they were in trouble.
10. ____Hicks; told Jamal to act more like a young man
12. Randy's age
13. Setting of the novel
17. ____ Haven; Randy was in prison there
18. Mr. ____ was Randy's lawyer.
20. Mama's ailment
22. Tito's grandmother
23. ____ Rodriguez wanted to borrow fifteen cents from Jamal or Tito.
24. Turned Randy in to a cop a plea.
25. What Mack gave Jamal

Down
1. Miss ____; Jamal's favorite teacher
2. Gave the gun to Jamal
3. Wondered if Jamal 'had the heart'
5. Didn't like Dwayne; gave him a disgusted look
6. Mrs. Rich said Jamal might spend another year in ____ grade.
7. Jerry ____; roughest kid in the school
9. Mack's age
11. Last name of boy who raced down the stairs in school with Jamal
14. Said Jamal didn't have any experience
15. Jamal's older brother who was in jail
16. ____Garvey; name of the park
19. Jamal pulled the gun on him during a fight.
20. Boat ____; Jamal and Tito liked to visit this place.
21. Jamal liked to ____ and paint.

Scorpions Word Search 4 Answer Key

		1 B	L	O	O	D		2 M			
		R			3 I		4 A	S	T	H	5 M	A
6 S	C	O	R	P	I	O	N	S		4 C			Y
	E		W				D		7 W		K			R
	V		N			8 E	I	G	H	T		9 S	I	N	G	H
	E						A		A			I		A
	N			10 J	E	V	O	N		11 L		V		X
	T						12 S	E	V	E	N	T	E	E	N
13 H	14 A	R	L	E	M				Y		L		E		
	N				15 R				A		E			16 M
17 G	R	E	E	N	18 A	D	19 D	I	S	O	N			A
	E						N		W		Q		20 B	U	R	N
	L		21 D			D		22 A	B	U	E	L	A			C
		R		Y		Y		E		S		U
23 C	E	L	I	A				N		Z		I		S
		24 W	I	L	L	I	E		25 G	U	N		

Across
1. First to notice Jamal's gun
4. Tito's ailment
6. Randy used to be their leader.
8. Sassy's age
9. Kids were sent to Mr. ____ if they were in trouble.
10. ____Hicks; told Jamal to act more like a young man
12. Randy's age
13. Setting of the novel
17. ____ Haven; Randy was in prison there
18. Mr. ____ was Randy's lawyer.
20. Mama's ailment
22. Tito's grandmother
23. ____ Rodriguez wanted to borrow fifteen cents from Jamal or Tito.
24. Turned Randy in to a cop a plea.
25. What Mack gave Jamal

Down
1. Miss ____; Jamal's favorite teacher
2. Gave the gun to Jamal
3. Wondered if Jamal 'had the heart'
5. Didn't like Dwayne; gave him a disgusted look
6. Mrs. Rich said Jamal might spend another year in ____ grade.
7. Jerry ____; roughest kid in the school
9. Mack's age
11. Last name of boy who raced down the stairs in school with Jamal
14. Said Jamal didn't have any experience
15. Jamal's older brother who was in jail
16. ____Garvey; name of the park
19. Jamal pulled the gun on him during a fight.
20. Boat ____; Jamal and Tito liked to visit this place.
21. Jamal liked to ____ and paint.

Scorpions

BURN	RICH	RANDY	GUN	SIXTEEN
DAVIDSON	MITCHELL	ANGEL	TITO	HARLEM
FOURTEEN	FIVE	FREE SPACE	SEVENTEEN	HICKS
ADDISON	BASIN	DRAW	INDIAN	ASTHMA
PUERTO	WILLIE	WHALEY	TWO	FIREHOUSE

Scorpions

EIGHT	BOATS	JEVON	SEVENTH	GONZALEZ
DWAYNE	STANTON	SPOFFORD	BIGGS	ROBERTS
SINGH	OSWALDO	FREE SPACE	MARCUS	MYRNA
TWELVE	BROWN	DARNELL	SCORPIONS	GREEN
ABUELA	DRAWING	CATHOLIC	BLOOD	MACK

Scorpions

DRAWING	CATHOLIC	ROBERTS	ASTHMA	CELIA
FIREHOUSE	ADDISON	TWO	TWELVE	OSWALDO
ANGEL	HARLEM	FREE SPACE	JEVON	MITCHELL
SPOFFORD	BASIN	BURN	FIVE	GUN
RANDY	BLOOD	TITO	PUERTO	RICH

Scorpions

DAVIDSON	DWAYNE	SEVENTH	HICKS	SEVENTEEN
VELASQUEZ	BROWN	BIGGS	STANTON	ABUELA
FOURTEEN	MARCUS	FREE SPACE	BOATS	WILLIE
EIGHT	WHALEY	GREEN	SINGH	DARNELL
DRAW	GONZALEZ	MACK	MYRNA	SIXTEEN

Scorpions

DRAWING	VELASQUEZ	GONZALEZ	ANGEL	FIVE
SCORPIONS	INDIAN	BIGGS	FOURTEEN	TWO
JEVON	GREEN	FREE SPACE	GUN	BURN
ROBERTS	RANDY	ABUELA	DARNELL	CATHOLIC
BROWN	TWELVE	MYRNA	HARLEM	PUERTO

Scorpions

SIXTEEN	BASIN	DRAW	TITO	WILLIE
MITCHELL	BLOOD	SINGH	BOATS	SEVENTEEN
RICH	SEVENTH	FREE SPACE	ADDISON	DWAYNE
FIREHOUSE	SPOFFORD	DAVIDSON	OSWALDO	MARCUS
HICKS	STANTON	EIGHT	MACK	CELIA

Scorpions

DWAYNE	SIXTEEN	GUN	MACK	INDIAN
FOURTEEN	TWO	RANDY	STANTON	DARNELL
GONZALEZ	EIGHT	FREE SPACE	MITCHELL	ANGEL
OSWALDO	FIVE	TWELVE	DRAWING	DAVIDSON
JEVON	HARLEM	BURN	VELASQUEZ	MARCUS

Scorpions

SINGH	CELIA	BASIN	SCORPIONS	FIREHOUSE
BLOOD	DRAW	ABUELA	SPOFFORD	BIGGS
BROWN	ASTHMA	FREE SPACE	WILLIE	SEVENTH
ADDISON	BOATS	MYRNA	HICKS	GREEN
RICH	ROBERTS	PUERTO	CATHOLIC	SEVENTEEN

Scorpions

TWO	MACK	FOURTEEN	WHALEY	SINGH
SEVENTEEN	MITCHELL	SIXTEEN	ABUELA	ANGEL
RANDY	OSWALDO	FREE SPACE	SEVENTH	GUN
RICH	VELASQUEZ	STANTON	SCORPIONS	PUERTO
ASTHMA	BURN	SPOFFORD	ROBERTS	GONZALEZ

Scorpions

BIGGS	ADDISON	DARNELL	DWAYNE	TITO
FIREHOUSE	INDIAN	DRAWING	DRAW	DAVIDSON
CATHOLIC	BASIN	FREE SPACE	WILLIE	FIVE
BOATS	CELIA	MARCUS	MYRNA	GREEN
HARLEM	BROWN	EIGHT	BLOOD	JEVON

Scorpions

JEVON	GUN	OSWALDO	WHALEY	ADDISON
DARNELL	FOURTEEN	MACK	TWELVE	SPOFFORD
CELIA	ABUELA	FREE SPACE	BIGGS	ANGEL
MYRNA	DAVIDSON	GREEN	BURN	DRAW
DRAWING	ASTHMA	TITO	HICKS	ROBERTS

Scorpions

BASIN	SINGH	SIXTEEN	INDIAN	GONZALEZ
DWAYNE	BOATS	SEVENTH	STANTON	RICH
PUERTO	FIREHOUSE	FREE SPACE	SCORPIONS	RANDY
WILLIE	MITCHELL	BROWN	FIVE	VELASQUEZ
SEVENTEEN	HARLEM	MARCUS	CATHOLIC	TWO

Scorpions

DARNELL	BROWN	EIGHT	MITCHELL	ROBERTS
TITO	BURN	SEVENTEEN	MACK	DAVIDSON
SIXTEEN	GREEN	FREE SPACE	SINGH	TWO
PUERTO	DWAYNE	BOATS	MARCUS	HICKS
OSWALDO	SCORPIONS	FOURTEEN	BIGGS	DRAW

Scorpions

TWELVE	GUN	ASTHMA	SPOFFORD	HARLEM
WILLIE	MYRNA	FIREHOUSE	BASIN	BLOOD
RICH	SEVENTH	FREE SPACE	STANTON	JEVON
CATHOLIC	INDIAN	GONZALEZ	VELASQUEZ	CELIA
ADDISON	WHALEY	FIVE	DRAWING	ABUELA

Scorpions

RANDY	WILLIE	DAVIDSON	ABUELA	ASTHMA
TITO	TWO	SIXTEEN	MITCHELL	RICH
BROWN	DARNELL	FREE SPACE	VELASQUEZ	HICKS
STANTON	ROBERTS	BLOOD	GREEN	SINGH
FIVE	BURN	WHALEY	EIGHT	BOATS

Scorpions

DWAYNE	JEVON	MACK	ANGEL	SCORPIONS
FIREHOUSE	MYRNA	DRAWING	OSWALDO	ADDISON
FOURTEEN	HARLEM	FREE SPACE	BIGGS	INDIAN
CATHOLIC	GUN	MARCUS	GONZALEZ	SEVENTEEN
CELIA	SEVENTH	SPOFFORD	TWELVE	PUERTO

Scorpions

CATHOLIC	MARCUS	HICKS	TWO	MACK
RICH	GREEN	HARLEM	EIGHT	OSWALDO
FIREHOUSE	ABUELA	FREE SPACE	VELASQUEZ	MITCHELL
SEVENTH	MYRNA	TITO	BLOOD	SEVENTEEN
DRAWING	DWAYNE	WHALEY	BROWN	ANGEL

Scorpions

SPOFFORD	BURN	WILLIE	SINGH	CELIA
DAVIDSON	ASTHMA	JEVON	SCORPIONS	GONZALEZ
ROBERTS	DARNELL	FREE SPACE	PUERTO	BIGGS
RANDY	BASIN	TWELVE	FIVE	STANTON
FOURTEEN	BOATS	GUN	DRAW	SIXTEEN

Scorpions

DRAW	FIVE	RICH	ROBERTS	HICKS
INDIAN	GONZALEZ	JEVON	BROWN	TITO
BURN	DARNELL	FREE SPACE	WHALEY	SPOFFORD
TWELVE	STANTON	MITCHELL	DAVIDSON	DRAWING
MACK	ANGEL	BIGGS	WILLIE	CELIA

Scorpions

SEVENTEEN	MARCUS	ADDISON	SINGH	SEVENTH
TWO	RANDY	BOATS	CATHOLIC	BASIN
MYRNA	ASTHMA	FREE SPACE	BLOOD	SCORPIONS
GUN	ABUELA	FIREHOUSE	PUERTO	DWAYNE
FOURTEEN	HARLEM	SIXTEEN	OSWALDO	VELASQUEZ

Scorpions

ADDISON	RANDY	RICH	SCORPIONS	BOATS
ABUELA	FOURTEEN	ROBERTS	TWO	FIVE
GREEN	ANGEL	FREE SPACE	PUERTO	EIGHT
DAVIDSON	BLOOD	TWELVE	BASIN	DWAYNE
INDIAN	SEVENTEEN	BIGGS	DRAW	DARNELL

Scorpions

STANTON	JEVON	VELASQUEZ	SIXTEEN	GONZALEZ
MACK	MYRNA	HARLEM	MITCHELL	WILLIE
TITO	BROWN	FREE SPACE	CELIA	MARCUS
ASTHMA	OSWALDO	WHALEY	FIREHOUSE	BURN
SEVENTH	SPOFFORD	CATHOLIC	DRAWING	GUN

Scorpions

BROWN	INDIAN	STANTON	DAVIDSON	TWO
BURN	DARNELL	ABUELA	ASTHMA	RANDY
MYRNA	FIREHOUSE	FREE SPACE	OSWALDO	BASIN
ROBERTS	ADDISON	JEVON	DRAW	WILLIE
GREEN	SCORPIONS	SEVENTEEN	HARLEM	FOURTEEN

Scorpions

RICH	SINGH	SIXTEEN	BIGGS	EIGHT
HICKS	GUN	CELIA	PUERTO	MITCHELL
BOATS	SEVENTH	FREE SPACE	VELASQUEZ	MACK
WHALEY	DRAWING	TITO	CATHOLIC	DWAYNE
MARCUS	FIVE	TWELVE	ANGEL	BLOOD

Scorpions

BROWN	WILLIE	CATHOLIC	HARLEM	ABUELA
DAVIDSON	GONZALEZ	ROBERTS	DARNELL	JEVON
VELASQUEZ	SEVENTEEN	FREE SPACE	SINGH	BURN
MARCUS	MITCHELL	DRAW	PUERTO	FIREHOUSE
FIVE	SPOFFORD	TWO	BIGGS	SCORPIONS

Scorpions

SEVENTH	ANGEL	OSWALDO	BOATS	STANTON
MACK	ASTHMA	DWAYNE	CELIA	INDIAN
BASIN	WHALEY	FREE SPACE	DRAWING	BLOOD
MYRNA	RICH	TWELVE	EIGHT	RANDY
GUN	TITO	ADDISON	HICKS	GREEN

Scorpions

GREEN	BIGGS	BOATS	ANGEL	DWAYNE
FIVE	MARCUS	EIGHT	TWO	PUERTO
BROWN	SPOFFORD	FREE SPACE	SCORPIONS	DAVIDSON
MITCHELL	GUN	STANTON	MACK	SINGH
GONZALEZ	SIXTEEN	FOURTEEN	ABUELA	WHALEY

Scorpions

RANDY	DARNELL	HARLEM	ASTHMA	DRAWING
SEVENTEEN	BASIN	INDIAN	CELIA	VELASQUEZ
CATHOLIC	BLOOD	FREE SPACE	WILLIE	MYRNA
TITO	OSWALDO	JEVON	SEVENTH	DRAW
BURN	RICH	ADDISON	TWELVE	ROBERTS

Scorpions

HICKS	BROWN	DAVIDSON	GREEN	JEVON
BASIN	FIVE	DRAWING	BOATS	GUN
SPOFFORD	ABUELA	FREE SPACE	ANGEL	STANTON
CATHOLIC	PUERTO	BIGGS	DWAYNE	OSWALDO
VELASQUEZ	BLOOD	WILLIE	MACK	ADDISON

Scorpions

TWO	SEVENTH	MITCHELL	FOURTEEN	MARCUS
ROBERTS	SCORPIONS	CELIA	ASTHMA	FIREHOUSE
INDIAN	GONZALEZ	FREE SPACE	SIXTEEN	SEVENTEEN
EIGHT	RANDY	SINGH	HARLEM	WHALEY
DARNELL	RICH	DRAW	TITO	MYRNA

Scorpions

MYRNA	RICH	STANTON	DAVIDSON	BLOOD
BIGGS	TITO	FOURTEEN	HARLEM	FIVE
TWO	SEVENTEEN	FREE SPACE	BROWN	INDIAN
TWELVE	ADDISON	CELIA	DRAWING	MARCUS
SEVENTH	EIGHT	WHALEY	FIREHOUSE	VELASQUEZ

Scorpions

ROBERTS	CATHOLIC	ASTHMA	DRAW	OSWALDO
RANDY	HICKS	GREEN	ABUELA	BASIN
ANGEL	PUERTO	FREE SPACE	JEVON	BOATS
GUN	MACK	GONZALEZ	SIXTEEN	DARNELL
MITCHELL	SPOFFORD	SINGH	DWAYNE	SCORPIONS

Scorpions Vocabulary Word List

No.	Word	Clue/Definition
1.	ACCUSATIONS	Charges of wrongdoing
2.	ANXIOUS	Fearful; panicky
3.	APPEAL	A request for a new court hearing
4.	AROMA	A pleasant odor
5.	BANNISTER	A handrail
6.	BECKONED	Made a signaling gesture
7.	BOBBING	Moving up and down
8.	CLENCHED	Closed tightly
9.	COMPARTMENT	A small room or section
10.	CONTAMINATE	To make impure
11.	DELINQUENT	Someone who disobeys the law
12.	DROOPED	Bent or sagged downward
13.	DROOPY	Sagging in exhaustion
14.	EPISODE	One part of a serial story or show
15.	GLANCED	Gazed briefly
16.	GLISTEN	Shine
17.	GRAVELLY	Sounding harsh or rasping
18.	HASTY	Rapidly; quickly
19.	JUVENILE	For or about children or young people
20.	LINGERED	Persisted; stayed
21.	MUSTY	Stale or moldy
22.	PAROLE	Supervised freedom from prison
23.	PEER	To look or search
24.	PIER	A platform over the water
25.	POLLUTION	Harmful waste matter
26.	POSSESSION	Holding without ownership
27.	PROJECTS	Government funded housing for the poor
28.	REFLECTIONS	Images
29.	SHIELD	A piece of armor strapped to the arm
30.	SLICK	Shrewd; tricky
31.	SLITS	Long, narrow openings
32.	SQUAT	Low and broad
33.	STAMMERED	Spoke with involuntary pauses
34.	STOCKY	Solidly built; sturdy
35.	STOOP	A building's small porch or staircase
36.	STRUT	A swaggering walk
37.	STUMBLED	Tripped
38.	SUBWAY	An underground, electric railway
39.	SULLENLY	With silent resentment
40.	TENEMENTS	Run-down apartment buildings
41.	VAGUELY	Not clearly expressed
42.	VIALS	Small containers with stoppers
43.	YACHT	A small boat used for cruises

Scorpions Vocabulary Fill In The Blanks 1

_____ 1. Someone who disobeys the law

_____ 2. A piece of armor strapped to the arm

_____ 3. Charges of wrongdoing

_____ 4. A platform over the water

_____ 5. Small containers with stoppers

_____ 6. A pleasant odor

_____ 7. Solidly built; sturdy

_____ 8. One part of a serial story or show

_____ 9. Persisted; stayed

_____ 10. Gazed briefly

_____ 11. Bent or sagged downward

_____ 12. Harmful waste matter

_____ 13. Shrewd; tricky

_____ 14. A small room or section

_____ 15. Made a signaling gesture

_____ 16. A building's small porch or staircase

_____ 17. Government funded housing for the poor

_____ 18. Long, narrow openings

_____ 19. Run-down apartment buildings

_____ 20. For or about children or young people

Scorpions Vocabulary Fill In The Blanks 1 Answer Key

DELINQUENT	1. Someone who disobeys the law
SHIELD	2. A piece of armor strapped to the arm
ACCUSATIONS	3. Charges of wrongdoing
PIER	4. A platform over the water
VIALS	5. Small containers with stoppers
AROMA	6. A pleasant odor
STOCKY	7. Solidly built; sturdy
EPISODE	8. One part of a serial story or show
LINGERED	9. Persisted; stayed
GLANCED	10. Gazed briefly
DROOPED	11. Bent or sagged downward
POLLUTION	12. Harmful waste matter
SLICK	13. Shrewd; tricky
COMPARTMENT	14. A small room or section
BECKONED	15. Made a signaling gesture
STOOP	16. A building's small porch or staircase
PROJECTS	17. Government funded housing for the poor
SLITS	18. Long, narrow openings
TENEMENTS	19. Run-down apartment buildings
JUVENILE	20. For or about children or young people

Scorpions Vocabulary Fill In The Blanks 2

_____ 1. A small room or section

_____ 2. Images

_____ 3. Tripped

_____ 4. Someone who disobeys the law

_____ 5. Government funded housing for the poor

_____ 6. Stale or moldy

_____ 7. Fearful; panicky

_____ 8. Solidly built; sturdy

_____ 9. A handrail

_____ 10. Sagging in exhaustion

_____ 11. A request for a new court hearing

_____ 12. Bent or sagged downward

_____ 13. Shine

_____ 14. Sounding harsh or rasping

_____ 15. Harmful waste matter

_____ 16. A piece of armor strapped to the arm

_____ 17. Supervised freedom from prison

_____ 18. Moving up and down

_____ 19. Low and broad

_____ 20. A building's small porch or staircase

Scorpions Vocabulary Fill In The Blanks 2 Answer Key

COMPARTMENT	1. A small room or section
REFLECTIONS	2. Images
STUMBLED	3. Tripped
DELINQUENT	4. Someone who disobeys the law
PROJECTS	5. Government funded housing for the poor
MUSTY	6. Stale or moldy
ANXIOUS	7. Fearful; panicky
STOCKY	8. Solidly built; sturdy
BANNISTER	9. A handrail
DROOPY	10. Sagging in exhaustion
APPEAL	11. A request for a new court hearing
DROOPED	12. Bent or sagged downward
GLISTEN	13. Shine
GRAVELLY	14. Sounding harsh or rasping
POLLUTION	15. Harmful waste matter
SHIELD	16. A piece of armor strapped to the arm
PAROLE	17. Supervised freedom from prison
BOBBING	18. Moving up and down
SQUAT	19. Low and broad
STOOP	20. A building's small porch or staircase

Scorpions Vocabulary Fill In The Blanks 3

_____   1. Closed tightly
_____   2. Made a signaling gesture
_____   3. Images
_____   4. One part of a serial story or show
_____   5. Government funded housing for the poor
_____   6. Shine
_____   7. Small containers with stoppers
_____   8. A small room or section
_____   9. A handrail
_____   10. A small boat used for cruises
_____   11. To look or search
_____   12. Harmful waste matter
_____   13. Low and broad
_____   14. A request for a new court hearing
_____   15. Holding without ownership
_____   16. An underground, electric railway
_____   17. Someone who disobeys the law
_____   18. Shrewd; tricky
_____   19. A piece of armor strapped to the arm
_____   20. Persisted; stayed

Scorpions Vocabulary Fill In The Blanks 3 Answer Key

CLENCHED	1. Closed tightly
BECKONED	2. Made a signaling gesture
REFLECTIONS	3. Images
EPISODE	4. One part of a serial story or show
PROJECTS	5. Government funded housing for the poor
GLISTEN	6. Shine
VIALS	7. Small containers with stoppers
COMPARTMENT	8. A small room or section
BANNISTER	9. A handrail
YACHT	10. A small boat used for cruises
PEER	11. To look or search
POLLUTION	12. Harmful waste matter
SQUAT	13. Low and broad
APPEAL	14. A request for a new court hearing
POSSESSION	15. Holding without ownership
SUBWAY	16. An underground, electric railway
DELINQUENT	17. Someone who disobeys the law
SLICK	18. Shrewd; tricky
SHIELD	19. A piece of armor strapped to the arm
LINGERED	20. Persisted; stayed

Scorpions Vocabulary Fill In The Blanks 4

1. A request for a new court hearing
2. Harmful waste matter
3. One part of a serial story or show
4. Someone who disobeys the law
5. Long, narrow openings
6. Moving up and down
7. Supervised freedom from prison
8. Tripped
9. Government funded housing for the poor
10. Sounding harsh or rasping
11. A swaggering walk
12. Not clearly expressed
13. Shrewd; tricky
14. A small boat used for cruises
15. Solidly built; sturdy
16. A building's small porch or staircase
17. Closed tightly
18. An underground, electric railway
19. Small containers with stoppers
20. Stale or moldy

Scorpions Vocabulary Fill In The Blanks 4 Answer Key

APPEAL	1. A request for a new court hearing
POLLUTION	2. Harmful waste matter
EPISODE	3. One part of a serial story or show
DELINQUENT	4. Someone who disobeys the law
SLITS	5. Long, narrow openings
BOBBING	6. Moving up and down
PAROLE	7. Supervised freedom from prison
STUMBLED	8. Tripped
PROJECTS	9. Government funded housing for the poor
GRAVELLY	10. Sounding harsh or rasping
STRUT	11. A swaggering walk
VAGUELY	12. Not clearly expressed
SLICK	13. Shrewd; tricky
YACHT	14. A small boat used for cruises
STOCKY	15. Solidly built; sturdy
STOOP	16. A building's small porch or staircase
CLENCHED	17. Closed tightly
SUBWAY	18. An underground, electric railway
VIALS	19. Small containers with stoppers
MUSTY	20. Stale or moldy

Scorpions Vocabulary Matching 1

___ 1. POLLUTION   A. Sounding harsh or rasping
___ 2. JUVENILE   B. Charges of wrongdoing
___ 3. BOBBING   C. Supervised freedom from prison
___ 4. SUBWAY   D. Moving up and down
___ 5. BECKONED   E. Holding without ownership
___ 6. CLENCHED   F. For or about children or young people
___ 7. GRAVELLY   G. To make impure
___ 8. ACCUSATIONS   H. A pleasant odor
___ 9. STOCKY   I. Small containers with stoppers
___10. PIER   J. One part of a serial story or show
___11. PEER   K. Low and broad
___12. MUSTY   L. Harmful waste matter
___13. VIALS   M. Bent or sagged downward
___14. TENEMENTS   N. Stale or moldy
___15. PAROLE   O. A platform over the water
___16. CONTAMINATE   P. Rapidly; quickly
___17. SLICK   Q. Solidly built; sturdy
___18. AROMA   R. Long, narrow openings
___19. POSSESSION   S. To look or search
___20. SLITS   T. An underground, electric railway
___21. SQUAT   U. Shrewd; tricky
___22. EPISODE   V. A swaggering walk
___23. HASTY   W. Closed tightly
___24. DROOPED   X. Made a signaling gesture
___25. STRUT   Y. Run-down apartment buildings

Scorpions Vocabulary Matching 1 Answer Key

L - 1. POLLUTION		A. Sounding harsh or rasping
F - 2. JUVENILE		B. Charges of wrongdoing
D - 3. BOBBING		C. Supervised freedom from prison
T - 4. SUBWAY		D. Moving up and down
X - 5. BECKONED		E. Holding without ownership
W - 6. CLENCHED		F. For or about children or young people
A - 7. GRAVELLY		G. To make impure
B - 8. ACCUSATIONS		H. A pleasant odor
Q - 9. STOCKY		I. Small containers with stoppers
O - 10. PIER		J. One part of a serial story or show
S - 11. PEER		K. Low and broad
N - 12. MUSTY		L. Harmful waste matter
I - 13. VIALS		M. Bent or sagged downward
Y - 14. TENEMENTS		N. Stale or moldy
C - 15. PAROLE		O. A platform over the water
G - 16. CONTAMINATE		P. Rapidly; quickly
U - 17. SLICK		Q. Solidly built; sturdy
H - 18. AROMA		R. Long, narrow openings
E - 19. POSSESSION		S. To look or search
R - 20. SLITS		T. An underground, electric railway
K - 21. SQUAT		U. Shrewd; tricky
J - 22. EPISODE		V. A swaggering walk
P - 23. HASTY		W. Closed tightly
M - 24. DROOPED		X. Made a signaling gesture
V - 25. STRUT		Y. Run-down apartment buildings

Scorpions Vocabulary Matching 2

___ 1. STUMBLED   A. Not clearly expressed
___ 2. STRUT   B. A small room or section
___ 3. DROOPED   C. A platform over the water
___ 4. PIER   D. Shine
___ 5. CONTAMINATE   E. Bent or sagged downward
___ 6. MUSTY   F. A request for a new court hearing
___ 7. ACCUSATIONS   G. Images
___ 8. APPEAL   H. Charges of wrongdoing
___ 9. POSSESSION   I. Stale or moldy
___10. POLLUTION   J. A swaggering walk
___11. SULLENLY   K. To make impure
___12. SUBWAY   L. Holding without ownership
___13. VAGUELY   M. Moving up and down
___14. STOCKY   N. Harmful waste matter
___15. STOOP   O. A handrail
___16. GLISTEN   P. With silent resentment
___17. BANNISTER   Q. Rapidly; quickly
___18. HASTY   R. One part of a serial story or show
___19. PEER   S. Persisted; stayed
___20. BOBBING   T. An underground, electric railway
___21. LINGERED   U. To look or search
___22. REFLECTIONS   V. Solidly built; sturdy
___23. EPISODE   W. Tripped
___24. DROOPY   X. A building's small porch or staircase
___25. COMPARTMENT   Y. Sagging in exhaustion

Scorpions Vocabulary Matching 2 Answer Key

W - 1.	STUMBLED	A.	Not clearly expressed
J - 2.	STRUT	B.	A small room or section
E - 3.	DROOPED	C.	A platform over the water
C - 4.	PIER	D.	Shine
K - 5.	CONTAMINATE	E.	Bent or sagged downward
I - 6.	MUSTY	F.	A request for a new court hearing
H - 7.	ACCUSATIONS	G.	Images
F - 8.	APPEAL	H.	Charges of wrongdoing
L - 9.	POSSESSION	I.	Stale or moldy
N - 10.	POLLUTION	J.	A swaggering walk
P - 11.	SULLENLY	K.	To make impure
T - 12.	SUBWAY	L.	Holding without ownership
A - 13.	VAGUELY	M.	Moving up and down
V - 14.	STOCKY	N.	Harmful waste matter
X - 15.	STOOP	O.	A handrail
D - 16.	GLISTEN	P.	With silent resentment
O - 17.	BANNISTER	Q.	Rapidly; quickly
Q - 18.	HASTY	R.	One part of a serial story or show
U - 19.	PEER	S.	Persisted; stayed
M - 20.	BOBBING	T.	An underground, electric railway
S - 21.	LINGERED	U.	To look or search
G - 22.	REFLECTIONS	V.	Solidly built; sturdy
R - 23.	EPISODE	W.	Tripped
Y - 24.	DROOPY	X.	A building's small porch or staircase
B - 25.	COMPARTMENT	Y.	Sagging in exhaustion

Scorpions Vocabulary Matching 3

___ 1. VAGUELY   A. Government funded housing for the poor
___ 2. DELINQUENT   B. Closed tightly
___ 3. VIALS   C. Shrewd; tricky
___ 4. STRUT   D. A swaggering walk
___ 5. MUSTY   E. A small room or section
___ 6. ANXIOUS   F. Made a signaling gesture
___ 7. STUMBLED   G. Solidly built; sturdy
___ 8. PAROLE   H. A small boat used for cruises
___ 9. DROOPED   I. Supervised freedom from prison
___ 10. HASTY   J. Holding without ownership
___ 11. GLANCED   K. Stale or moldy
___ 12. SLICK   L. For or about children or young people
___ 13. APPEAL   M. To make impure
___ 14. PROJECTS   N. Fearful; panicky
___ 15. AROMA   O. Shine
___ 16. GLISTEN   P. Someone who disobeys the law
___ 17. CLENCHED   Q. A request for a new court hearing
___ 18. BECKONED   R. Tripped
___ 19. CONTAMINATE   S. Small containers with stoppers
___ 20. STOCKY   T. Gazed briefly
___ 21. POSSESSION   U. Not clearly expressed
___ 22. BANNISTER   V. A pleasant odor
___ 23. COMPARTMENT   W. Bent or sagged downward
___ 24. JUVENILE   X. Rapidly; quickly
___ 25. YACHT   Y. A handrail

Scorpions Vocabulary Matching 3 Answer Key

U -	1. VAGUELY	A.	Government funded housing for the poor
P -	2. DELINQUENT	B.	Closed tightly
S -	3. VIALS	C.	Shrewd; tricky
D -	4. STRUT	D.	A swaggering walk
K -	5. MUSTY	E.	A small room or section
N -	6. ANXIOUS	F.	Made a signaling gesture
R -	7. STUMBLED	G.	Solidly built; sturdy
I -	8. PAROLE	H.	A small boat used for cruises
W -	9. DROOPED	I.	Supervised freedom from prison
X -	10. HASTY	J.	Holding without ownership
T -	11. GLANCED	K.	Stale or moldy
C -	12. SLICK	L.	For or about children or young people
Q -	13. APPEAL	M.	To make impure
A -	14. PROJECTS	N.	Fearful; panicky
V -	15. AROMA	O.	Shine
O -	16. GLISTEN	P.	Someone who disobeys the law
B -	17. CLENCHED	Q.	A request for a new court hearing
F -	18. BECKONED	R.	Tripped
M -	19. CONTAMINATE	S.	Small containers with stoppers
G -	20. STOCKY	T.	Gazed briefly
J -	21. POSSESSION	U.	Not clearly expressed
Y -	22. BANNISTER	V.	A pleasant odor
E -	23. COMPARTMENT	W.	Bent or sagged downward
L -	24. JUVENILE	X.	Rapidly; quickly
H -	25. YACHT	Y.	A handrail

Scorpions Vocabulary Matching 4

___ 1. BANNISTER   A. A pleasant odor
___ 2. HASTY   B. A request for a new court hearing
___ 3. APPEAL   C. With silent resentment
___ 4. LINGERED   D. Made a signaling gesture
___ 5. COMPARTMENT   E. Bent or sagged downward
___ 6. SHIELD   F. Closed tightly
___ 7. STOOP   G. A swaggering walk
___ 8. PROJECTS   H. Supervised freedom from prison
___ 9. PAROLE   I. Rapidly; quickly
___10. PEER   J. Low and broad
___11. SQUAT   K. A handrail
___12. DROOPED   L. Harmful waste matter
___13. YACHT   M. An underground, electric railway
___14. BOBBING   N. Sounding harsh or rasping
___15. GRAVELLY   O. Persisted; stayed
___16. SULLENLY   P. Government funded housing for the poor
___17. SUBWAY   Q. Moving up and down
___18. CLENCHED   R. A piece of armor strapped to the arm
___19. AROMA   S. A building's small porch or staircase
___20. STRUT   T. To look or search
___21. BECKONED   U. A small room or section
___22. POLLUTION   V. Shrewd; tricky
___23. VAGUELY   W. Tripped
___24. STUMBLED   X. A small boat used for cruises
___25. SLICK   Y. Not clearly expressed

Scorpions Vocabulary Matching 4 Answer Key

K - 1. BANNISTER   A. A pleasant odor
I - 2. HASTY   B. A request for a new court hearing
B - 3. APPEAL   C. With silent resentment
O - 4. LINGERED   D. Made a signaling gesture
U - 5. COMPARTMENT   E. Bent or sagged downward
R - 6. SHIELD   F. Closed tightly
S - 7. STOOP   G. A swaggering walk
P - 8. PROJECTS   H. Supervised freedom from prison
H - 9. PAROLE   I. Rapidly; quickly
T - 10. PEER   J. Low and broad
J - 11. SQUAT   K. A handrail
E - 12. DROOPED   L. Harmful waste matter
X - 13. YACHT   M. An underground, electric railway
Q - 14. BOBBING   N. Sounding harsh or rasping
N - 15. GRAVELLY   O. Persisted; stayed
C - 16. SULLENLY   P. Government funded housing for the poor
M - 17. SUBWAY   Q. Moving up and down
F - 18. CLENCHED   R. A piece of armor strapped to the arm
A - 19. AROMA   S. A building's small porch or staircase
G - 20. STRUT   T. To look or search
D - 21. BECKONED   U. A small room or section
L - 22. POLLUTION   V. Shrewd; tricky
Y - 23. VAGUELY   W. Tripped
W - 24. STUMBLED   X. A small boat used for cruises
V - 25. SLICK   Y. Not clearly expressed

Scorpions Vocabulary Magic Squares 1

Match the definition with the vocabulary word. Put your answers in the magic squares below. When your answers are correct, all columns and rows will add to the same number.

A. LINGERED
B. REFLECTIONS
C. PAROLE
D. VAGUELY
E. DROOPY
F. GRAVELLY
G. YACHT
H. EPISODE
I. HASTY
J. AROMA
K. POLLUTION
L. CONTAMINATE
M. SQUAT
N. SLITS
O. GLISTEN
P. JUVENILE

1. One part of a serial story or show
2. Persisted; stayed
3. Images
4. A small boat used for cruises
5. A pleasant odor
6. Shine
7. For or about children or young people
8. Rapidly; quickly
9. Harmful waste matter
10. Long, narrow openings
11. Low and broad
12. To make impure
13. Sagging in exhaustion
14. Not clearly expressed
15. Supervised freedom from prison
16. Sounding harsh or rasping

A=	B=	C=	D=
E=	F=	G=	H=
I=	J=	K=	L=
M=	N=	O=	P=

Scorpions Vocabulary Magic Squares 1 Answer Key

Match the definition with the vocabulary word. Put your answers in the magic squares below. When your answers are correct, all columns and rows will add to the same number.

A. LINGERED E. DROOPY I. HASTY M. SQUAT
B. REFLECTIONS F. GRAVELLY J. AROMA N. SLITS
C. PAROLE G. YACHT K. POLLUTION O. GLISTEN
D. VAGUELY H. EPISODE L. CONTAMINATE P. JUVENILE

1. One part of a serial story or show
2. Persisted; stayed
3. Images
4. A small boat used for cruises
5. A pleasant odor
6. Shine
7. For or about children or young people
8. Rapidly; quickly
9. Harmful waste matter
10. Long, narrow openings
11. Low and broad
12. To make impure
13. Sagging in exhaustion
14. Not clearly expressed
15. Supervised freedom from prison
16. Sounding harsh or rasping

A=2	B=3	C=15	D=14
E=13	F=16	G=4	H=1
I=8	J=5	K=9	L=12
M=11	N=10	O=6	P=7

79
Copyrighted

Scorpions Vocabulary Magic Squares 2

Match the definition with the vocabulary word. Put your answers in the magic squares below. When your answers are correct, all columns and rows will add to the same number.

A. STOCKY
B. JUVENILE
C. SQUAT
D. GLISTEN
E. POLLUTION
F. STUMBLED
G. PIER
H. REFLECTIONS
I. EPISODE
J. SUBWAY
K. AROMA
L. LINGERED
M. TENEMENTS
N. VIALS
O. BOBBING
P. VAGUELY

1. For or about children or young people
2. A platform over the water
3. A pleasant odor
4. Small containers with stoppers
5. Run-down apartment buildings
6. Persisted; stayed
7. Images
8. Solidly built; sturdy
9. Not clearly expressed
10. One part of a serial story or show
11. Harmful waste matter
12. Shine
13. Low and broad
14. Tripped
15. An underground, electric railway
16. Moving up and down

A=	B=	C=	D=
E=	F=	G=	H=
I=	J=	K=	L=
M=	N=	O=	P=

Scorpions Vocabulary Magic Squares 2 Answer Key

Match the definition with the vocabulary word. Put your answers in the magic squares below. When your answers are correct, all columns and rows will add to the same number.

A. STOCKY	E. POLLUTION	I. EPISODE	M. TENEMENTS
B. JUVENILE	F. STUMBLED	J. SUBWAY	N. VIALS
C. SQUAT	G. PIER	K. AROMA	O. BOBBING
D. GLISTEN	H. REFLECTIONS	L. LINGERED	P. VAGUELY

1. For or about children or young people
2. A platform over the water
3. A pleasant odor
4. Small containers with stoppers
5. Run-down apartment buildings
6. Persisted; stayed
7. Images
8. Solidly built; sturdy
9. Not clearly expressed
10. One part of a serial story or show
11. Harmful waste matter
12. Shine
13. Low and broad
14. Tripped
15. An underground, electric railway
16. Moving up and down

A=8	B=1	C=13	D=12
E=11	F=14	G=2	H=7
I=10	J=15	K=3	L=6
M=5	N=4	O=16	P=9

Scorpions Vocabulary Magic Squares 3

Match the definition with the vocabulary word. Put your answers in the magic squares below. When your answers are correct, all columns and rows will add to the same number.

A. STRUT
B. ANXIOUS
C. STAMMERED
D. CONTAMINATE
E. DROOPED
F. BECKONED
G. BOBBING
H. APPEAL
I. SUBWAY
J. DELINQUENT
K. PROJECTS
L. HASTY
M. PEER
N. DROOPY
O. TENEMENTS
P. SULLENLY

1. To look or search
2. Made a signaling gesture
3. A request for a new court hearing
4. Run-down apartment buildings
5. Rapidly; quickly
6. Spoke with involuntary pauses
7. A swaggering walk
8. Someone who disobeys the law
9. Government funded housing for the poor
10. To make impure
11. Fearful; panicky
12. An underground, electric railway
13. Sagging in exhaustion
14. Bent or sagged downward
15. Moving up and down
16. With silent resentment

A=	B=	C=	D=
E=	F=	G=	H=
I=	J=	K=	L=
M=	N=	O=	P=

Scorpions Vocabulary Magic Squares 3 Answer Key

Match the definition with the vocabulary word. Put your answers in the magic squares below. When your answers are correct, all columns and rows will add to the same number.

A. STRUT	E. DROOPED	I. SUBWAY	M. PEER
B. ANXIOUS	F. BECKONED	J. DELINQUENT	N. DROOPY
C. STAMMERED	G. BOBBING	K. PROJECTS	O. TENEMENTS
D. CONTAMINATE	H. APPEAL	L. HASTY	P. SULLENLY

1. To look or search
2. Made a signaling gesture
3. A request for a new court hearing
4. Run-down apartment buildings
5. Rapidly; quickly
6. Spoke with involuntary pauses
7. A swaggering walk
8. Someone who disobeys the law
9. Government funded housing for the poor
10. To make impure
11. Fearful; panicky
12. An underground, electric railway
13. Sagging in exhaustion
14. Bent or sagged downward
15. Moving up and down
16. With silent resentment

A=7	B=11	C=6	D=10
E=14	F=2	G=15	H=3
I=12	J=8	K=9	L=5
M=1	N=13	O=4	P=16

Scorpions Vocabulary Magic Squares 4

Match the definition with the vocabulary word. Put your answers in the magic squares below. When your answers are correct, all columns and rows will add to the same number.

A. DELINQUENT   E. STUMBLED   I. POLLUTION   M. YACHT
B. STOOP   F. EPISODE   J. STRUT   N. DROOPY
C. STOCKY   G. SULLENLY   K. CONTAMINATE O. GLANCED
D. PEER   H. STAMMERED L. TENEMENTS   P. GRAVELLY

1. Spoke with involuntary pauses
2. A small boat used for cruises
3. A building's small porch or staircase
4. To make impure
5. A swaggering walk
6. Solidly built; sturdy
7. Sounding harsh or rasping
8. Tripped
9. Gazed briefly
10. One part of a serial story or show
11. Harmful waste matter
12. To look or search
13. Someone who disobeys the law
14. Run-down apartment buildings
15. With silent resentment
16. Sagging in exhaustion

A=	B=	C=	D=
E=	F=	G=	H=
I=	J=	K=	L=
M=	N=	O=	P=

Scorpions Vocabulary Magic Squares 4 Answer Key

Match the definition with the vocabulary word. Put your answers in the magic squares below. When your answers are correct, all columns and rows will add to the same number.

A. DELINQUENT   E. STUMBLED   I. POLLUTION   M. YACHT
B. STOOP   F. EPISODE   J. STRUT   N. DROOPY
C. STOCKY   G. SULLENLY   K. CONTAMINATE   O. GLANCED
D. PEER   H. STAMMERED   L. TENEMENTS   P. GRAVELLY

1. Spoke with involuntary pauses
2. A small boat used for cruises
3. A building's small porch or staircase
4. To make impure
5. A swaggering walk
6. Solidly built; sturdy
7. Sounding harsh or rasping
8. Tripped
9. Gazed briefly
10. One part of a serial story or show
11. Harmful waste matter
12. To look or search
13. Someone who disobeys the law
14. Run-down apartment buildings
15. With silent resentment
16. Sagging in exhaustion

A=13	B=3	C=6	D=12
E=8	F=10	G=15	H=1
I=11	J=5	K=4	L=14
M=2	N=16	O=9	P=7

Scorpions Vocabulary Word Search 1

Words are placed backwards, forward, diagonally, up and down. Clues listed below can help you find the words. Circle the hidden vocabulary words in the maze.

S	N	O	I	T	A	S	U	C	C	A	S	T	U	M	B	L	E	D	V
T	T	S	L	M	D	U	T	W	Q	L	L	T	K	R	G	G	W	E	V
O	M	O	O	C	N	B	H	G	A	K	I	C	R	Q	V	L	T	N	C
C	D	R	O	X	W	W	X	I	G	N	T	L	X	U	S	I	N	O	G
K	A	R	S	P	J	A	V	H	N	H	S	E	G	Y	T	S	H	K	B
Y	Z	T	O	P	N	Y	K	O	I	H	Q	N	N	Z	W	T	B	C	Z
C	H	N	J	O	S	M	I	L	B	Z	N	C	N	E	Y	E	D	E	S
N	O	B	X	B	P	S	B	I	B	N	K	H	X	Z	M	N	R	B	Y
K	T	N	M	G	S	E	E	N	O	D	C	E	N	D	D	E	Z	L	Y
C	D	N	T	E	R	D	D	G	B	G	K	D	G	E	F	P	N	Z	Q
W	F	N	S	A	O	A	H	E	N	F	P	P	R	R	S	E	B	T	B
C	D	S	F	S	M	J	V	R	F	S	S	E	J	N	L	L	B	M	S
Z	O	E	I	K	B	I	Q	E	F	G	M	G	O	L	F	V	J	S	W
P	K	P	L	L	A	G	N	D	L	M	D	I	U	C	R	J	Z	L	P
C	E	K	L	I	N	B	G	A	A	L	T	S	R	T	P	C	M	P	K
O	F	M	F	F	N	V	P	T	T	C	Y	B	H	R	C	S	R	X	D
M	M	J	W	K	I	Q	S	O	E	E	F	Y	M	Q	Z	O	C	M	C
P	G	B	U	Y	S	N	U	L	L	G	Q	A	G	R	J	S	V	W	T
A	L	Z	N	V	T	V	F	E	D	L	C	C	G	E	Y	F	W	A	F
R	A	N	B	V	E	E	A	H	N	D	U	H	C	I	S	W	U	N	C
T	N	P	E	E	R	N	Q	G	Y	T	R	T	M	P	Z	Q	V	X	P
M	C	J	V	Y	J	H	I	T	U	Y	S	O	I	U	S	D	H	I	X
E	E	W	L	F	R	C	S	L	B	E	C	S	O	O	S	M	D	O	N
N	D	E	L	O	R	A	P	P	E	A	L	T	R	P	N	T	G	U	G
T	D	L	E	I	H	S	S	L	I	C	K	Y	M	N	Y	M	Y	S	B

A building's small porch or staircase (5)
A handrail (9)
A piece of armor strapped to the arm (6)
A platform over the water (4)
A pleasant odor (5)
A request for a new court hearing (6)
A small boat used for cruises (5)
A small room or section (11)
A swaggering walk (5)
An underground, electric railway (6)
Bent or sagged downward (7)
Charges of wrongdoing (11)
Closed tightly (8)
Fearful; panicky (7)
For or about children or young people (8)
Gazed briefly (7)
Government funded housing for the poor (8)
Harmful waste matter (9)
Holding without ownership (10)
Images (11)
Long, narrow openings (5)
Low and broad (5)

Made a signaling gesture (8)
Moving up and down (7)
Not clearly expressed (7)
One part of a serial story or show (7)
Persisted; stayed (8)
Rapidly; quickly (5)
Run-down apartment buildings (9)
Sagging in exhaustion (6)
Shine (7)
Shrewd; tricky (5)
Small containers with stoppers (5)
Solidly built; sturdy (6)
Someone who disobeys the law (10)
Sounding harsh or rasping (8)
Spoke with involuntary pauses (9)
Stale or moldy (5)
Supervised freedom from prison (6)
To look or search (4)
To make impure (11)
Tripped (8)
With silent resentment (8)

Scorpions Vocabulary Word Search 1 Answer Key

Words are placed backwards, forward, diagonally, up and down. Clues listed below can help you find the words. Circle the hidden vocabulary words in the maze.

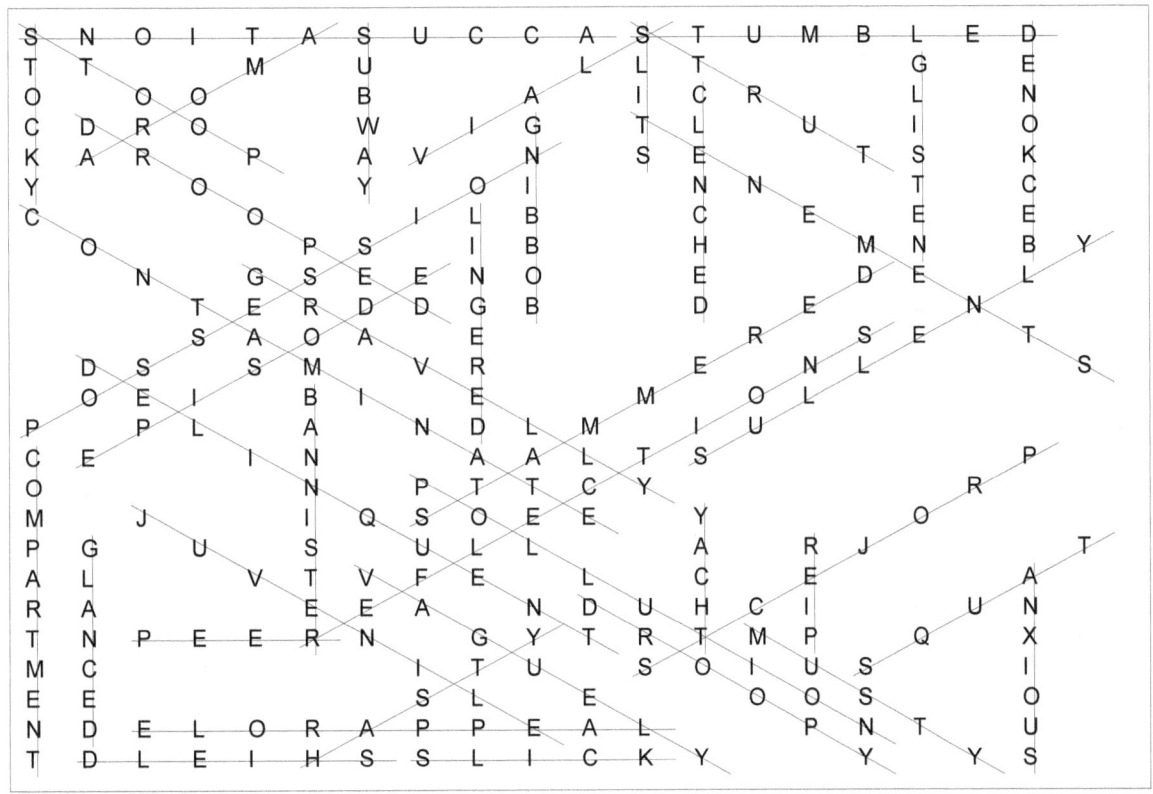

A building's small porch or staircase (5)
A handrail (9)
A piece of armor strapped to the arm (6)
A platform over the water (4)
A pleasant odor (5)
A request for a new court hearing (6)
A small boat used for cruises (5)
A small room or section (11)
A swaggering walk (5)
An underground, electric railway (6)
Bent or sagged downward (7)
Charges of wrongdoing (11)
Closed tightly (8)
Fearful; panicky (7)
For or about children or young people (8)
Gazed briefly (7)
Government funded housing for the poor (8)
Harmful waste matter (9)
Holding without ownership (10)
Images (11)
Long, narrow openings (5)
Low and broad (5)

Made a signaling gesture (8)
Moving up and down (7)
Not clearly expressed (7)
One part of a serial story or show (7)
Persisted; stayed (8)
Rapidly; quickly (5)
Run-down apartment buildings (9)
Sagging in exhaustion (6)
Shine (7)
Shrewd; tricky (5)
Small containers with stoppers (5)
Solidly built; sturdy (6)
Someone who disobeys the law (10)
Sounding harsh or rasping (8)
Spoke with involuntary pauses (9)
Stale or moldy (5)
Supervised freedom from prison (6)
To look or search (4)
To make impure (11)
Tripped (8)
With silent resentment (8)

Scorpions Vocabulary Word Search 2

Words are placed backwards, forward, diagonally, up and down. Clues listed below can help you find the words. Circle the hidden vocabulary words in the maze.

```
G W F B G Y G M S D G F M D S Y T L A H
D M F V Y T P R N H L P Q U N U I N R D
K R R S Q E R C D S A J E V S N B M O N
Z Z O N L D P L E S N D P E G T D W M Q
B E D O S I P E R T C P I E R S Y H A W
P Y R I P N N N E U E T R L A T B A B Y
T A P T X E N C M M D E V I V O O S A L
P D R C T T D H M B D N A N E O B T N X
H R O E A P P E A L V E G E L P B Y N V
N O J L U O O D T E I M U V L R I A I S
Y O E F Q L S S S D A E E U Y V N C S H
H P C E S L U Y S R L N L J S Z G H T D
X Y T R D U L T G E S T Y G L W Q T E R
L B S L H T L S H H S S T N I P C L R A
S C F X Q I E R I J S N N T G I C C S
B L Z H H O N E G K W E I Y S N S C O V
V C I L H N L T U R T S L O Q H U B M R
Q S G C M D Y R M S U N M U N S Y E P K
R G J B K Y F H I O S W E F A J P C A M
F W Y N N Y G L I P H N W T T G W K R C
D C Y H K W G X Y D T W I H B J D O T Z
B B N C D H N S L Z Y O Q X Z R Y N M W
Z L O P T A N P R Y N V H G Z B Q E E K
L T Y T J C Q Y F S V L V T Y G N D N Q
S F W H C O N T A M I N A T E N Y Y T X
```

A building's small porch or staircase (5)
A handrail (9)
A piece of armor strapped to the arm (6)
A platform over the water (4)
A pleasant odor (5)
A request for a new court hearing (6)
A small boat used for cruises (5)
A small room or section (11)
A swaggering walk (5)
An underground, electric railway (6)
Bent or sagged downward (7)
Charges of wrongdoing (11)
Closed tightly (8)
Fearful; panicky (7)
For or about children or young people (8)
Gazed briefly (7)
Government funded housing for the poor (8)
Harmful waste matter (9)
Holding without ownership (10)
Images (11)
Long, narrow openings (5)
Low and broad (5)

Made a signaling gesture (8)
Moving up and down (7)
Not clearly expressed (7)
One part of a serial story or show (7)
Persisted; stayed (8)
Rapidly; quickly (5)
Run-down apartment buildings (9)
Sagging in exhaustion (6)
Shine (7)
Shrewd; tricky (5)
Small containers with stoppers (5)
Solidly built; sturdy (6)
Someone who disobeys the law (10)
Sounding harsh or rasping (8)
Spoke with involuntary pauses (9)
Stale or moldy (5)
Supervised freedom from prison (6)
To look or search (4)
To make impure (11)
Tripped (8)
With silent resentment (8)

Scorpions Vocabulary Word Search 2 Answer Key

Words are placed backwards, forward, diagonally, up and down. Clues listed below can help you find the words. Circle the hidden vocabulary words in the maze.

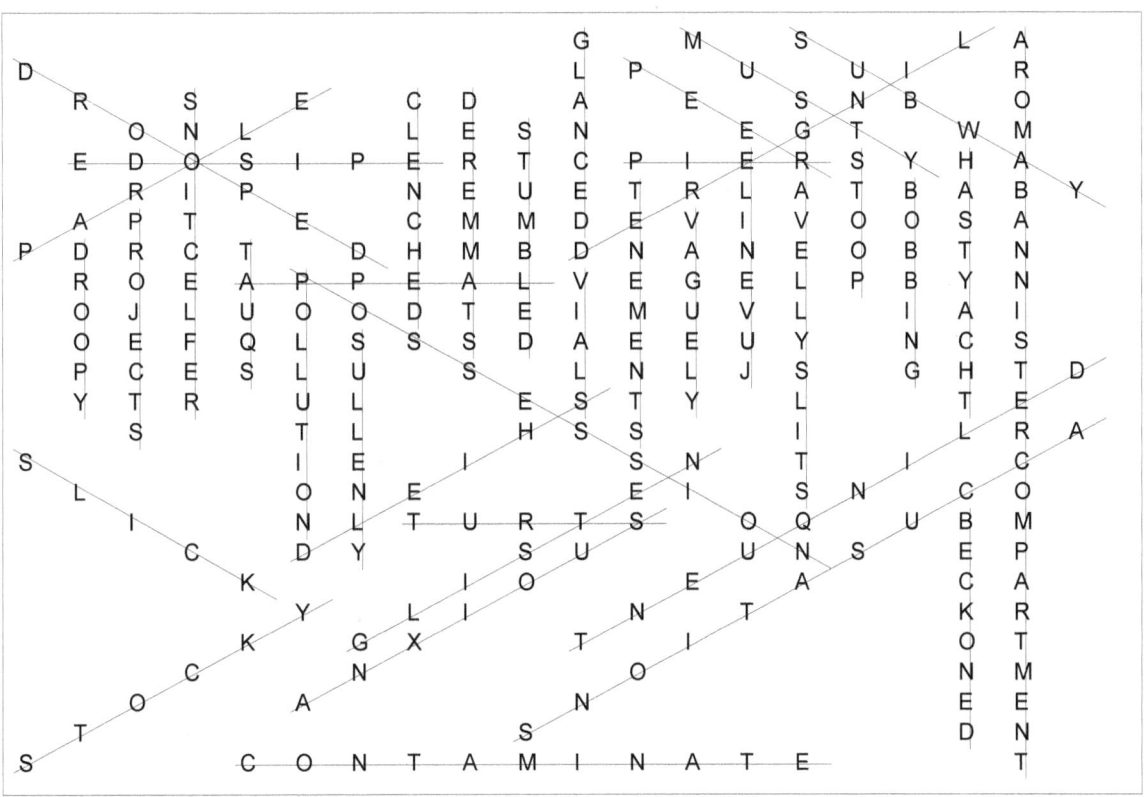

A building's small porch or staircase (5)
A handrail (9)
A piece of armor strapped to the arm (6)
A platform over the water (4)
A pleasant odor (5)
A request for a new court hearing (6)
A small boat used for cruises (5)
A small room or section (11)
A swaggering walk (5)
An underground, electric railway (6)
Bent or sagged downward (7)
Charges of wrongdoing (11)
Closed tightly (8)
Fearful; panicky (7)
For or about children or young people (8)
Gazed briefly (7)
Government funded housing for the poor (8)
Harmful waste matter (9)
Holding without ownership (10)
Images (11)
Long, narrow openings (5)
Low and broad (5)

Made a signaling gesture (8)
Moving up and down (7)
Not clearly expressed (7)
One part of a serial story or show (7)
Persisted; stayed (8)
Rapidly; quickly (5)
Run-down apartment buildings (9)
Sagging in exhaustion (6)
Shine (7)
Shrewd; tricky (5)
Small containers with stoppers (5)
Solidly built; sturdy (6)
Someone who disobeys the law (10)
Sounding harsh or rasping (8)
Spoke with involuntary pauses (9)
Stale or moldy (5)
Supervised freedom from prison (6)
To look or search (4)
To make impure (11)
Tripped (8)
With silent resentment (8)

89
Copyrighted

Scorpions Vocabulary Word Search 3

Words are placed backwards, forward, diagonally, up and down. Words listed below are included in the maze. Circle the hidden vocabulary words in the maze.

```
S U L L E N L Y D L E I H S E A B P P G
T C C I H O T J E V N C Y L L N O R A P
U O V N C I X G L S W T I D Y X B O R W
M M X G Q S Z Z I Q T N W A D I B J O L
B P S E K S B M N L E A W Q S O I E L F
L A P R P E C J Q V W B M N Q U N C E G
E R T E P S Q B U D U S O M G S G T J X
D T J D P S H J E S K I T Q E R D S A P
N M G N M O D N N V T J L G K R S X C R
N E K T M P O M T C E P X R B Y E C C C
V N Q C C K L L E T F G J X C T T D U H
B T S Y C Z M L A V G R A V E L L Y S D
C J B E D L F N N N H D V Y B G Q D A B
P L B C L E I N P T Y E R C M L L Y T Z
L J E J R M D X E D X P S S D I C X I D
P D D N A P L X E H R O T Z S S V T O T
G X E T C A M O R A P O L L U T I O N K
S L N P E H N M Y M C R O R Q E O J S Q
D O A R I N E L M K R D S P S N P O T Z
C M E N C S E D Y U V C S L Y Q Z R P X
L I R N C U O M T Q S I I T I R U J H H
P M H H G E C D E C K T A J R C P A A L
T H C A Y C D X E N S D Y L W U K S T C
B T V T M Q D P N T T M N Q S Z T B J M
A P P E A L B A N N I S T E R Y Y V Y Q
```

ACCUSATIONS	CONTAMINATE	JUVENILE	REFLECTIONS	STUMBLED
ANXIOUS	DELINQUENT	LINGERED	SHIELD	SUBWAY
APPEAL	DROOPED	MUSTY	SLICK	SULLENLY
AROMA	DROOPY	PAROLE	SLITS	TENEMENTS
BANNISTER	EPISODE	PEER	SQUAT	VAGUELY
BECKONED	GLANCED	PIER	STAMMERED	VIALS
BOBBING	GLISTEN	POLLUTION	STOCKY	YACHT
CLENCHED	GRAVELLY	POSSESSION	STOOP	
COMPARTMENT	HASTY	PROJECTS	STRUT	

Scorpions Vocabulary Word Search 3 Answer Key

Words are placed backwards, forward, diagonally, up and down. Words listed below are included in the maze. Circle the hidden vocabulary words in the maze.

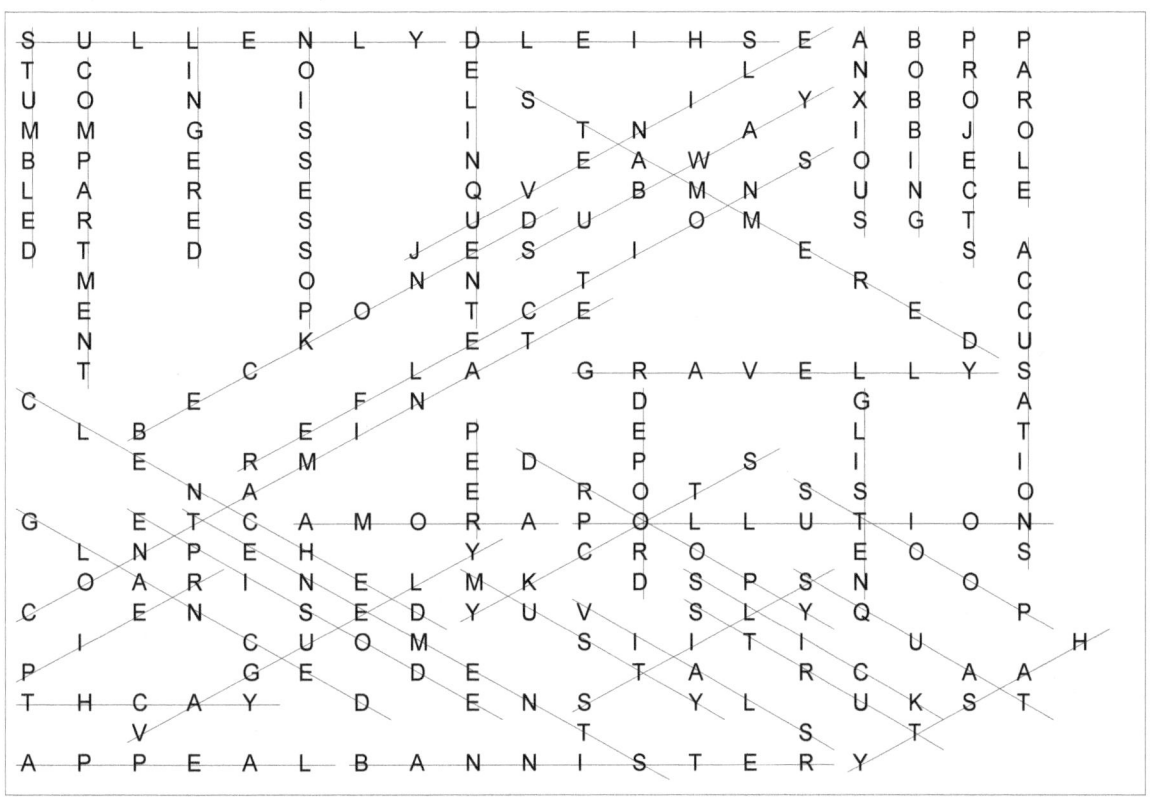

ACCUSATIONS	CONTAMINATE	JUVENILE	REFLECTIONS	STUMBLED
ANXIOUS	DELINQUENT	LINGERED	SHIELD	SUBWAY
APPEAL	DROOPED	MUSTY	SLICK	SULLENLY
AROMA	DROOPY	PAROLE	SLITS	TENEMENTS
BANNISTER	EPISODE	PEER	SQUAT	VAGUELY
BECKONED	GLANCED	PIER	STAMMERED	VIALS
BOBBING	GLISTEN	POLLUTION	STOCKY	YACHT
CLENCHED	GRAVELLY	POSSESSION	STOOP	
COMPARTMENT	HASTY	PROJECTS	STRUT	

Scorpions Vocabulary Word Search 4

Words are placed backwards, forward, diagonally, up and down. Words listed below are included in the maze. Circle the hidden vocabulary words in the maze.

```
P B M X C Q Y B D E L I N Q U E N T N S
O E X W Q O R P A X Y V S R C L R M E D
L C Y N H M M E X N V D N H N I S H T X
L K J L P K X P F V N Q T V I N P T S T
U O G V D E C N A L G I D E R E G N I L
T N H N F Q F G M R E S S J G V L F L P
I E P P C F F G K W T C T T K U Y D G Q
O D Q S Z J D V F H P M T O E J M F Z X
N D P O S S E S S I O N E I C R L P H B
R R R C C Q Z S T C K X H N O K L X D D
P V Y O Q X H U J V L J Q T T N Y J R L
X K A G O P T L Y L L E V A R G S Z R V
S H G G P P P L C C T V N Z P R F V X X
Q F N N U V Y E J M A W L C B Q S I P J
S D I R H E K N P L U C R F H T H A R G
G H B T K P L L X I Q N M B H E H L O J
S U B W A Y Z Y S S S L I C K A D S J Z
F E O L A X X T U T B O A K S P Q P E F
Y L B M Q W N O I A U Y D T T P H E C L
N O O M P E I L G M K M Y E R E G E T K
J R Y V M X S M G M S S B F U A M R S D
A A B E N Q S B U E P T Z L T L E N X D
B P N A T B B S G R P O J V E I L Y X G
K E J X W M T R L E T O P K P D G S N N
T B Q X B Y D K W D W P D R O O P E D P
```

ANXIOUS	DROOPED	MUSTY	SLICK	SULLENLY
APPEAL	DROOPY	PAROLE	SLITS	TENEMENTS
AROMA	EPISODE	PEER	SQUAT	VAGUELY
BANNISTER	GLANCED	PIER	STAMMERED	VIALS
BECKONED	GLISTEN	POLLUTION	STOCKY	YACHT
BOBBING	GRAVELLY	POSSESSION	STOOP	
CLENCHED	HASTY	PROJECTS	STRUT	
COMPARTMENT	JUVENILE	REFLECTIONS	STUMBLED	
DELINQUENT	LINGERED	SHIELD	SUBWAY	

Scorpions Vocabulary Word Search 4 Answer Key

Words are placed backwards, forward, diagonally, up and down. Words listed below are included in the maze. Circle the hidden vocabulary words in the maze.

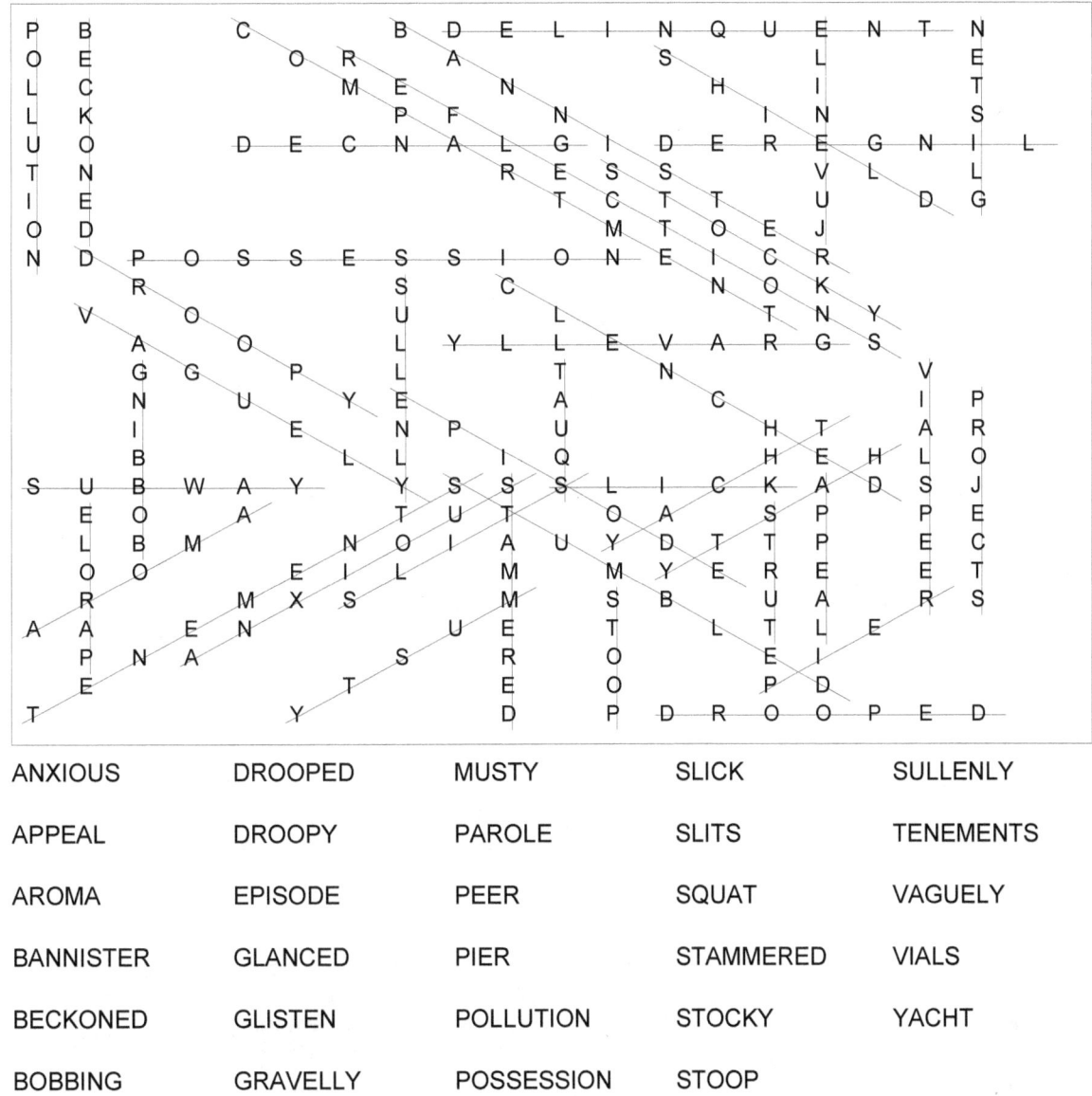

ANXIOUS	DROOPED	MUSTY	SLICK	SULLENLY
APPEAL	DROOPY	PAROLE	SLITS	TENEMENTS
AROMA	EPISODE	PEER	SQUAT	VAGUELY
BANNISTER	GLANCED	PIER	STAMMERED	VIALS
BECKONED	GLISTEN	POLLUTION	STOCKY	YACHT
BOBBING	GRAVELLY	POSSESSION	STOOP	
CLENCHED	HASTY	PROJECTS	STRUT	
COMPARTMENT	JUVENILE	REFLECTIONS	STUMBLED	
DELINQUENT	LINGERED	SHIELD	SUBWAY	

Scorpions Vocabulary Crossword 1

Across
2. Gazed briefly
5. Government funded housing for the poor
8. Solidly built; sturdy
10. Fearful; panicky
11. Made a signaling gesture
14. Rapidly; quickly
16. Shrewd; tricky
17. For or about children or young people
19. A pleasant odor
20. An underground, electric railway
21. A swaggering walk
22. Supervised freedom from prison
23. Not clearly expressed

Down
1. Holding without ownership
3. Charges of wrongdoing
4. Bent or sagged downward
5. A platform over the water
6. To make impure
7. Low and broad
8. Long, narrow openings
9. A small boat used for cruises
12. Closed tightly
13. One part of a serial story or show
15. To look or search
18. Small containers with stoppers
19. A request for a new court hearing
20. A building's small porch or staircase

Scorpions Vocabulary Crossword 1 Answer Key

		1 P						2 G	3 L	A	N	C	E	4 D
5 P	R	O	J	E	6 C	T	7 S			C				R
I		S			O		Q		8 S	T	O	C	9 Y	O
E		S			N		U		L		U		A	O
R		E			T		10 A	N	X	I	O	U	S	P
		S			A		T		T		S		C	H
		S			M				S				H	E
		I			I								T	D
		O			N			11 B	12 E	C	K	13 O	N	E	D
		N		14 H	A	S	T	Y		L		N		P	
				T				15 P		E		16 S	L	I	C	K
	17 J	18 U	V	E	N	I	L	E		N			S	
		I						E		C		19 A	R	O	M	A
20 S	U	B	W	A	Y			R		H		P		D	
T				L						E		P		E	
O				21 S	T	R	U	T		D		E		
O												A		
22 P	A	R	O	L	E			23 V	A	G	U	E	L	Y

Across
2. Gazed briefly
5. Government funded housing for the poor
8. Solidly built; sturdy
10. Fearful; panicky
11. Made a signaling gesture
14. Rapidly; quickly
16. Shrewd; tricky
17. For or about children or young people
19. A pleasant odor
20. An underground, electric railway
21. A swaggering walk
22. Supervised freedom from prison
23. Not clearly expressed

Down
1. Holding without ownership
3. Charges of wrongdoing
4. Bent or sagged downward
5. A platform over the water
6. To make impure
7. Low and broad
8. Long, narrow openings
9. A small boat used for cruises
12. Closed tightly
13. One part of a serial story or show
15. To look or search
18. Small containers with stoppers
19. A request for a new court hearing
20. A building's small porch or staircase

Scorpions Vocabulary Crossword 2

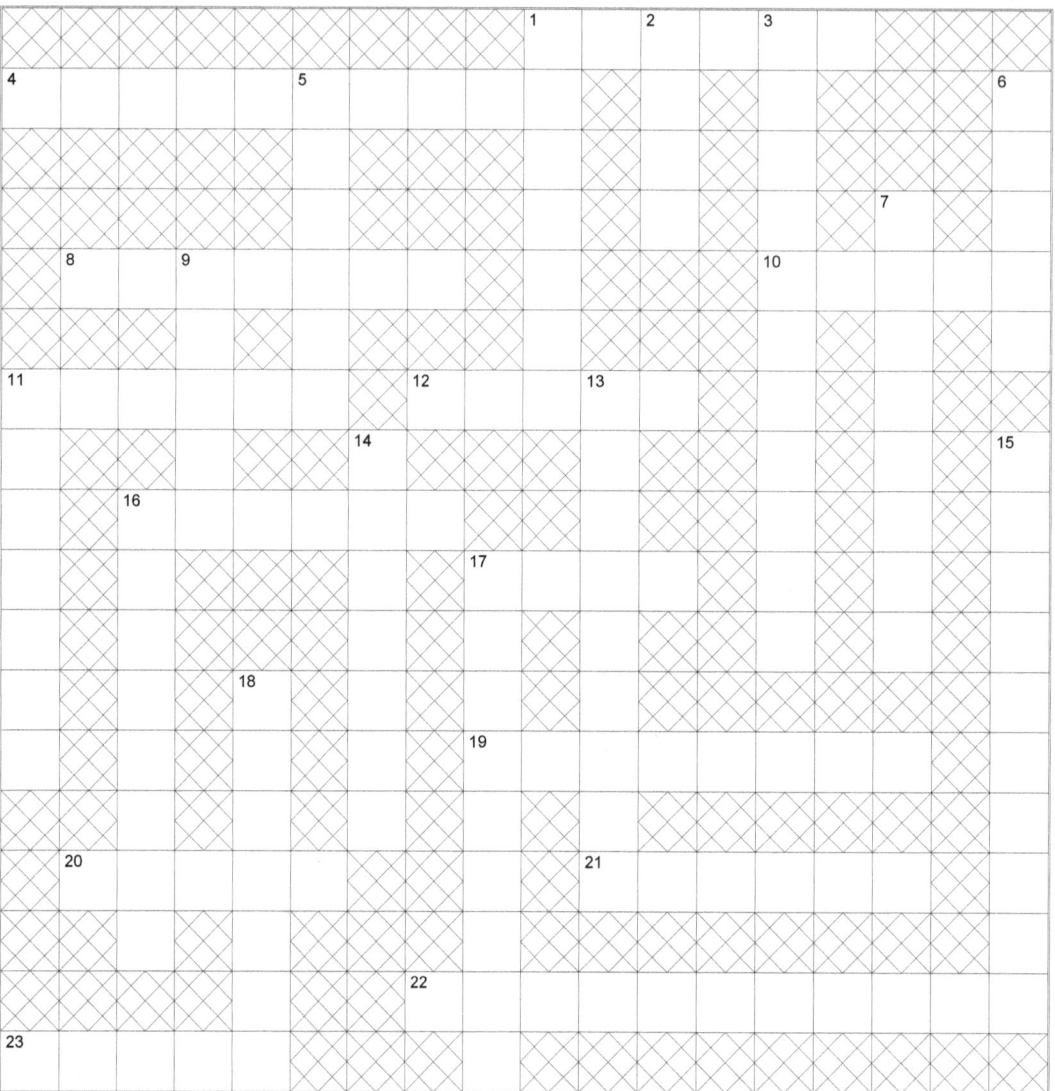

Across
1. A request for a new court hearing
4. Holding without ownership
8. Gazed briefly
10. Low and broad
11. Sagging in exhaustion
12. Rapidly; quickly
16. Supervised freedom from prison
17. To look or search
19. Persisted; stayed
20. A swaggering walk
21. An underground, electric railway
22. A small room or section
23. Stale or moldy

Down
1. Fearful; panicky
2. A platform over the water
3. Charges of wrongdoing
5. Solidly built; sturdy
6. Long, narrow openings
7. For or about children or young people
9. A pleasant odor
11. Bent or sagged downward
13. Run-down apartment buildings
14. Shine
15. Someone who disobeys the law
16. Government funded housing for the poor
17. Harmful waste matter
18. Not clearly expressed

Scorpions Vocabulary Crossword 2 Answer Key

Across
1. A request for a new court hearing
4. Holding without ownership
8. Gazed briefly
10. Low and broad
11. Sagging in exhaustion
12. Rapidly; quickly
16. Supervised freedom from prison
17. To look or search
19. Persisted; stayed
20. A swaggering walk
21. An underground, electric railway
22. A small room or section
23. Stale or moldy

Down
1. Fearful; panicky
2. A platform over the water
3. Charges of wrongdoing
5. Solidly built; sturdy
6. Long, narrow openings
7. For or about children or young people
9. A pleasant odor
11. Bent or sagged downward
13. Run-down apartment buildings
14. Shine
15. Someone who disobeys the law
16. Government funded housing for the poor
17. Harmful waste matter
18. Not clearly expressed

Scorpions Vocabulary Crossword 3

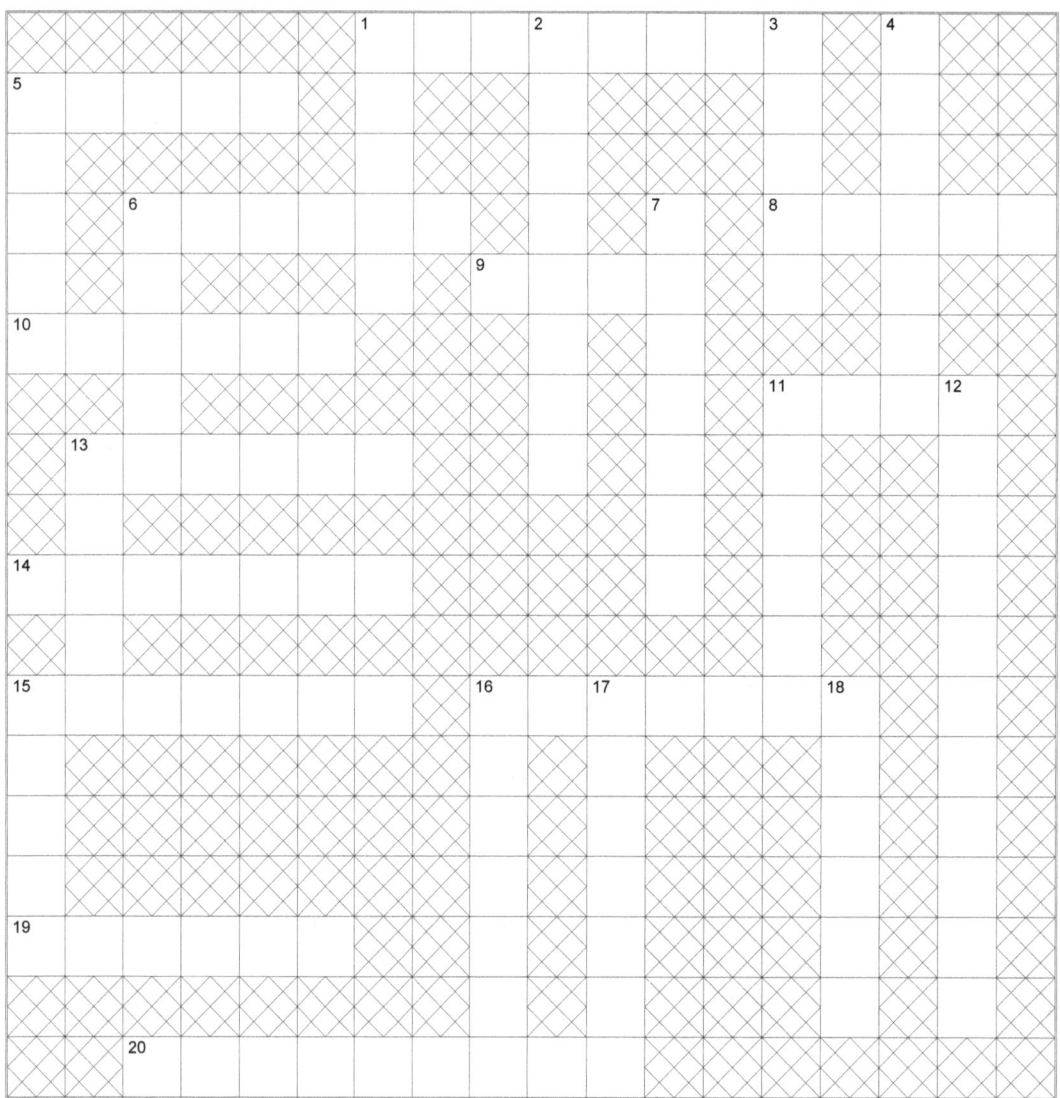

Across
1. With silent resentment
5. Shrewd; tricky
6. An underground, electric railway
8. Rapidly; quickly
9. To look or search
10. Solidly built; sturdy
11. A platform over the water
13. A request for a new court hearing
14. Moving up and down
15. Not clearly expressed
16. Gazed briefly
19. A piece of armor strapped to the arm
20. Run-down apartment buildings

Down
1. Low and broad
2. Persisted; stayed
3. A small boat used for cruises
4. One part of a serial story or show
5. Long, narrow openings
6. A building's small porch or staircase
7. Bent or sagged downward
11. Supervised freedom from prison
12. Images
13. A pleasant odor
15. Small containers with stoppers
16. Shine
17. Fearful; panicky
18. Sagging in exhaustion

Scorpions Vocabulary Crossword 3 Answer Key

					1 S	U	2 L	E	N	L	3 Y		4 E	
5 S	L	I	C	K	Q		I				A		P	
L					U		N			7	C		I	
I		6 S	U	B	W	A	Y		G	D	8 H	A	S	T	Y
T		T			T		9 P	E	E	R	T		O	
10 S	T	O	C	K	Y				R	O			D	
		O							E	O		11 P	I	12 E	R
		13 A	P	P	E	A	L		D		P	A		E
		R							E		R			F
14 B	O	B	B	I	N	G				D		O		L
		M										L		E
15 V	A	G	U	E	L	Y		16 G	17 L	A	N	C	18 E	D	C
I								L	N				R	T
A								I	X				O	I
L								S	I				O	O
19 S	H	I	E	L	D			T	O			P		N
								E	U			Y		S
		20 T	E	N	E	M	E	N	T	S				

Across
1. With silent resentment
5. Shrewd; tricky
6. An underground, electric railway
8. Rapidly; quickly
9. To look or search
10. Solidly built; sturdy
11. A platform over the water
13. A request for a new court hearing
14. Moving up and down
15. Not clearly expressed
16. Gazed briefly
19. A piece of armor strapped to the arm
20. Run-down apartment buildings

Down
1. Low and broad
2. Persisted; stayed
3. A small boat used for cruises
4. One part of a serial story or show
5. Long, narrow openings
6. A building's small porch or staircase
7. Bent or sagged downward
11. Supervised freedom from prison
12. Images
13. A pleasant odor
15. Small containers with stoppers
16. Shine
17. Fearful; panicky
18. Sagging in exhaustion

Scorpions Vocabulary Crossword 4

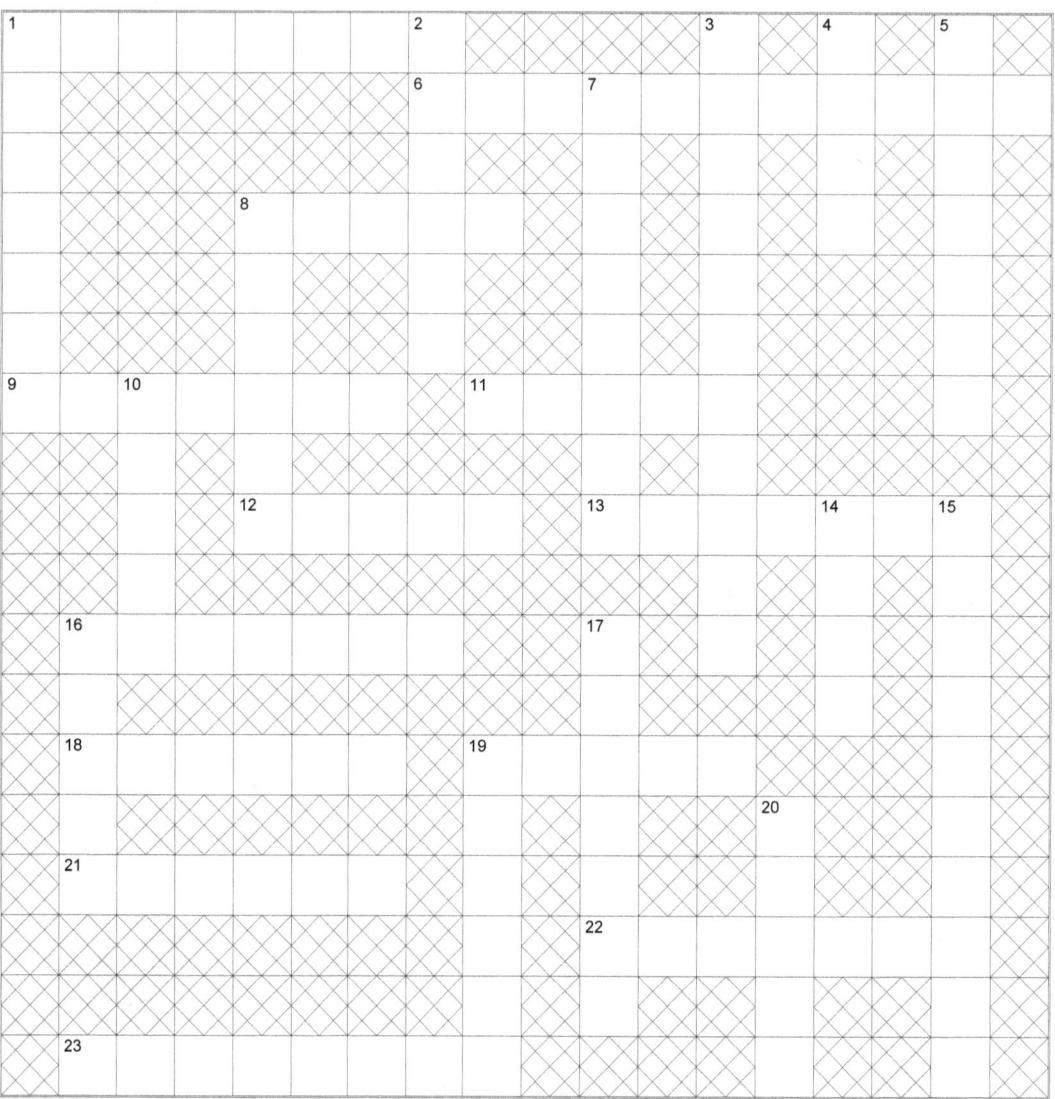

Across
1. Made a signaling gesture
6. Images
8. A building's small porch or staircase
9. Gazed briefly
11. A swaggering walk
12. A small boat used for cruises
13. Bent or sagged downward
16. Not clearly expressed
18. A request for a new court hearing
19. Long, narrow openings
21. A piece of armor strapped to the arm
22. One part of a serial story or show
23. With silent resentment

Down
1. Moving up and down
2. Sagging in exhaustion
3. Charges of wrongdoing
4. A platform over the water
5. Fearful; panicky
7. Persisted; stayed
8. Solidly built; sturdy
10. A pleasant odor
14. To look or search
15. Someone who disobeys the law
16. Small containers with stoppers
17. Shine
19. An underground, electric railway
20. Rapidly; quickly

Scorpions Vocabulary Crossword 4 Answer Key

	1 B	E	C	K	O	N	E	D	2 D			3 A		4 P		5 A	
	O								6 R	E	7 F	L	E	C	T	I	O	N	S
	B								O			I		C		E		X	
	B				8 S	T	O	O	P			N		U		R		I	
	I				T				P			G		S				O	
	N				O				Y			E		A				U	
9 G	L	10 A	N	C	E	D		11 S	T	R	U	T			S	
		R		K				E		I						
		O		12 Y	A	C	H	T		13 D	R	O	O	14 P	E	15 D
		M								O			E		E	
	16 V	A	G	U	E	L	Y		17 G			S		E		L
	I								L					R		I
	18 A	P	P	E	A	L		19 S	L	I	T	S				N
	L							U				20 H			Q
	21 S	H	I	E	L	D		B				A			U
								22 W	E	P	I	S	O	D	E
								A		N		T			N
	23 S	U	L	L	E	N	L	Y				Y			T

Across
1. Made a signaling gesture
6. Images
8. A building's small porch or staircase
9. Gazed briefly
11. A swaggering walk
12. A small boat used for cruises
13. Bent or sagged downward
16. Not clearly expressed
18. A request for a new court hearing
19. Long, narrow openings
21. A piece of armor strapped to the arm
22. One part of a serial story or show
23. With silent resentment

Down
1. Moving up and down
2. Sagging in exhaustion
3. Charges of wrongdoing
4. A platform over the water
5. Fearful; panicky
7. Persisted; stayed
8. Solidly built; sturdy
10. A pleasant odor
14. To look or search
15. Someone who disobeys the law
16. Small containers with stoppers
17. Shine
19. An underground, electric railway
20. Rapidly; quickly

Scorpions Vocabulary Juggle Letters 1

1. AVYRLELG = 1. _____
   Sounding harsh or rasping

2. OTPSO = 2. _____
   A building's small porch or staircase

3. LPLTUOOIN = 3. _____
   Harmful waste matter

4. TMYUS = 4. _____
   Stale or moldy

5. RSTTU = 5. _____
   A swaggering walk

6. OSYTKC = 6. _____
   Solidly built; sturdy

7. OCSFRETLNIE = 7. _____
   Images

8. DCANLGE = 8. _____
   Gazed briefly

9. LEDNCHCE = 9. _____
   Closed tightly

10. TEABNSRIN =10. _____
    A handrail

11. ISOSNOSPES =11. _____
    Holding without ownership

12. TSUAAONCICS =12. _____
    Charges of wrongdoing

13. LSTSI =13. _____
    Long, narrow openings

14. YVEGLUA =14. _____
    Not clearly expressed

15. TASYH =15. _____
    Rapidly; quickly

Copyrighted

Scorpions Vocabulary Juggle Letters 1 Answer Key

1. AVYRLELG = 1. GRAVELLY
   Sounding harsh or rasping

2. OTPSO = 2. STOOP
   A building's small porch or staircase

3. LPLTUOOIN = 3. POLLUTION
   Harmful waste matter

4. TMYUS = 4. MUSTY
   Stale or moldy

5. RSTTU = 5. STRUT
   A swaggering walk

6. OSYTKC = 6. STOCKY
   Solidly built; sturdy

7. OCSFRETLNIE = 7. REFLECTIONS
   Images

8. DCANLGE = 8. GLANCED
   Gazed briefly

9. LEDNCHCE = 9. CLENCHED
   Closed tightly

10. TEABNSRIN =10. BANNISTER
    A handrail

11. ISOSNOSPES =11. POSSESSION
    Holding without ownership

12. TSUAAONCICS =12. ACCUSATIONS
    Charges of wrongdoing

13. LSTSI =13. SLITS
    Long, narrow openings

14. YVEGLUA =14. VAGUELY
    Not clearly expressed

15. TASYH =15. HASTY
    Rapidly; quickly

Scorpions Vocabulary Juggle Letters 2

1. ROPELA = 1. _____
Supervised freedom from prison

2. RDEEINLG = 2. _____
Persisted; stayed

3. OEIENLSCTRF = 3. _____
Images

4. CDAGNLE = 4. _____
Gazed briefly

5. TAACONTMINE = 5. _____
To make impure

6. LGEYVUA = 6. _____
Not clearly expressed

7. QSTUA = 7. _____
Low and broad

8. OUISAXN = 8. _____
Fearful; panicky

9. CSILK = 9. _____
Shrewd; tricky

10. MDBTUELS = 10. _____
Tripped

11. TPCJEOSR = 11. _____
Government funded housing for the poor

12. LEUYNLLS = 12. _____
With silent resentment

13. ODDERPO = 13. _____
Bent or sagged downward

14. HENCECDL = 14. _____
Closed tightly

15. YTCOKS = 15. _____
Solidly built; sturdy

Scorpions Vocabulary Juggle Letters 2 Answer Key

1. ROPELA = 1. PAROLE
   Supervised freedom from prison

2. RDEEINLG = 2. LINGERED
   Persisted; stayed

3. OEIENLSCTRF = 3. REFLECTIONS
   Images

4. CDAGNLE = 4. GLANCED
   Gazed briefly

5. TAACONTMINE = 5. CONTAMINATE
   To make impure

6. LGEYVUA = 6. VAGUELY
   Not clearly expressed

7. QSTUA = 7. SQUAT
   Low and broad

8. OUISAXN = 8. ANXIOUS
   Fearful; panicky

9. CSILK = 9. SLICK
   Shrewd; tricky

10. MDBTUELS = 10. STUMBLED
    Tripped

11. TPCJEOSR = 11. PROJECTS
    Government funded housing for the poor

12. LEUYNLLS = 12. SULLENLY
    With silent resentment

13. ODDERPO = 13. DROOPED
    Bent or sagged downward

14. HENCECDL = 14. CLENCHED
    Closed tightly

15. YTCOKS = 15. STOCKY
    Solidly built; sturdy

Copyrighted

Scorpions Vocabulary Juggle Letters 3

1. EREP = 1. _____
   To look or search

2. QUAST = 2. _____
   Low and broad

3. EPSSSOONSI = 3. _____
   Holding without ownership

4. OTRCPSEJ = 4. _____
   Government funded housing for the poor

5. IREP = 5. _____
   A platform over the water

6. VLNUJEIE = 6. _____
   For or about children or young people

7. RCMTANTOMPE = 7. _____
   A small room or section

8. DEENOBCK = 8. _____
   Made a signaling gesture

9. TBSDMELU = 9. _____
   Tripped

10. ENTNTEEMS =10. _____
    Run-down apartment buildings

11. YDPOOR =11. _____
    Sagging in exhaustion

12. LAROPE =12. _____
    Supervised freedom from prison

13. RSDMMTAEE =13. _____
    Spoke with involuntary pauses

14. OSCLETFINRE =14. _____
    Images

15. AMRAO =15. _____
    A pleasant odor

Scorpions Vocabulary Juggle Letters 3 Answer Key

1. EREP = 1. PEER
   To look or search

2. QUAST = 2. SQUAT
   Low and broad

3. EPSSSOONSI = 3. POSSESSION
   Holding without ownership

4. OTRCPSEJ = 4. PROJECTS
   Government funded housing for the poor

5. IREP = 5. PIER
   A platform over the water

6. VLNUJEIE = 6. JUVENILE
   For or about children or young people

7. RCMTANTOMPE = 7. COMPARTMENT
   A small room or section

8. DEENOBCK = 8. BECKONED
   Made a signaling gesture

9. TBSDMELU = 9. STUMBLED
   Tripped

10. ENTNTEEMS = 10. TENEMENTS
    Run-down apartment buildings

11. YDPOOR = 11. DROOPY
    Sagging in exhaustion

12. LAROPE = 12. PAROLE
    Supervised freedom from prison

13. RSDMMTAEE = 13. STAMMERED
    Spoke with involuntary pauses

14. OSCLETFINRE = 14. REFLECTIONS
    Images

15. AMRAO = 15. AROMA
    A pleasant odor

Scorpions Vocabulary Juggle Letters 4

1. LVIEUEJN = 1. _____
   For or about children or young people

2. REPI = 2. _____
   A platform over the water

3. NASUOIX = 3. _____
   Fearful; panicky

4. BSTMUDEL = 4. _____
   Tripped

5. DTAEESRMM = 5. _____
   Spoke with involuntary pauses

6. NETIGLS = 6. _____
   Shine

7. ENESNMTTE = 7. _____
   Run-down apartment buildings

8. OSTPO = 8. _____
   A building's small porch or staircase

9. YMUTS = 9. _____
   Stale or moldy

10. UQSAT =10. _____
    Low and broad

11. SOEIDEP =11. _____
    One part of a serial story or show

12. DIELSH =12. _____
    A piece of armor strapped to the arm

13. ITCOMTNANEA =13. _____
    To make impure

14. DINRGEEL =14. _____
    Persisted; stayed

15. CNIAAUSTSCO =15. _____
    Charges of wrongdoing

Scorpions Vocabulary Juggle Letters 4 Answer Key

1. LVIEUEJN = 1. JUVENILE
   For or about children or young people

2. REPI = 2. PIER
   A platform over the water

3. NASUOIX = 3. ANXIOUS
   Fearful; panicky

4. BSTMUDEL = 4. STUMBLED
   Tripped

5. DTAEESRMM = 5. STAMMERED
   Spoke with involuntary pauses

6. NETIGLS = 6. GLISTEN
   Shine

7. ENESNMTTE = 7. TENEMENTS
   Run-down apartment buildings

8. OSTPO = 8. STOOP
   A building's small porch or staircase

9. YMUTS = 9. MUSTY
   Stale or moldy

10. UQSAT = 10. SQUAT
    Low and broad

11. SOEIDEP = 11. EPISODE
    One part of a serial story or show

12. DIELSH = 12. SHIELD
    A piece of armor strapped to the arm

13. ITCOMTNANEA = 13. CONTAMINATE
    To make impure

14. DINRGEEL = 14. LINGERED
    Persisted; stayed

15. CNIAAUSTSCO = 15. ACCUSATIONS
    Charges of wrongdoing

ACCUSATIONS	Charges of wrongdoing
ANXIOUS	Fearful; panicky
APPEAL	A request for a new court hearing
AROMA	A pleasant odor
BANNISTER	A handrail
BECKONED	Made a signaling gesture

BOBBING	Moving up and down
CLENCHED	Closed tightly
COMPARTMENT	A small room or section
CONTAMINATE	To make impure
DELINQUENT	Someone who disobeys the law
DROOPED	Bent or sagged downward

DROOPY	Sagging in exhaustion
EPISODE	One part of a serial story or show
GLANCED	Gazed briefly
GLISTEN	Shine
GRAVELLY	Sounding harsh or rasping
HASTY	Rapidly; quickly

JUVENILE	For or about children or young people
LINGERED	Persisted; stayed
MUSTY	Stale or moldy
PAROLE	Supervised freedom from prison
PEER	To look or search
PIER	A platform over the water

POLLUTION	Harmful waste matter
POSSESSION	Holding without ownership
PROJECTS	Government funded housing for the poor
REFLECTIONS	Images
SHIELD	A piece of armor strapped to the arm
SLICK	Shrewd; tricky

SLITS	Long, narrow openings
SQUAT	Low and broad
STAMMERED	Spoke with involuntary pauses
STOCKY	Solidly built; sturdy
STOOP	A building's small porch or staircase
STRUT	A swaggering walk

STUMBLED	Tripped
SUBWAY	An underground, electric railway
SULLENLY	With silent resentment
TENEMENTS	Run-down apartment buildings
VAGUELY	Not clearly expressed
VIALS	Small containers with stoppers

YACHT	A small boat used for cruises

Scorpions Vocabulary

STAMMERED	COMPARTMENT	SQUAT	POSSESSION	VAGUELY
TENEMENTS	PEER	STOOP	SULLENLY	ACCUSATIONS
SHIELD	GLANCED	FREE SPACE	DROOPY	STUMBLED
EPISODE	SLITS	APPEAL	BANNISTER	DROOPED
DELINQUENT	HASTY	JUVENILE	CONTAMINATE	PROJECTS

Scorpions Vocabulary

PIER	REFLECTIONS	SUBWAY	GLISTEN	LINGERED
GRAVELLY	VIALS	PAROLE	BOBBING	POLLUTION
STOCKY	SLICK	FREE SPACE	STRUT	ANXIOUS
MUSTY	AROMA	CLENCHED	PROJECTS	CONTAMINATE
JUVENILE	HASTY	DELINQUENT	DROOPED	BANNISTER

Scorpions Vocabulary

BANNISTER	STRUT	STAMMERED	DELINQUENT	DROOPY
PIER	GRAVELLY	BECKONED	HASTY	AROMA
REFLECTIONS	SULLENLY	FREE SPACE	COMPARTMENT	ACCUSATIONS
SUBWAY	POLLUTION	PEER	SQUAT	CONTAMINATE
YACHT	VAGUELY	PROJECTS	SHIELD	JUVENILE

Scorpions Vocabulary

EPISODE	POSSESSION	CLENCHED	SLITS	STOCKY
STUMBLED	APPEAL	DROOPED	STOOP	BOBBING
GLANCED	GLISTEN	FREE SPACE	LINGERED	PAROLE
MUSTY	TENEMENTS	ANXIOUS	JUVENILE	SHIELD
PROJECTS	VAGUELY	YACHT	CONTAMINATE	SQUAT

Scorpions Vocabulary

ACCUSATIONS	MUSTY	ANXIOUS	PIER	GLANCED
POSSESSION	APPEAL	AROMA	VIALS	SQUAT
PEER	CLENCHED	FREE SPACE	GLISTEN	COMPARTMENT
GRAVELLY	POLLUTION	STAMMERED	REFLECTIONS	DROOPY
STRUT	CONTAMINATE	SLITS	SHIELD	BOBBING

Scorpions Vocabulary

VAGUELY	SLICK	YACHT	SULLENLY	DELINQUENT
PAROLE	PROJECTS	EPISODE	SUBWAY	HASTY
TENEMENTS	STUMBLED	FREE SPACE	BECKONED	BANNISTER
STOOP	DROOPED	JUVENILE	BOBBING	SHIELD
SLITS	CONTAMINATE	STRUT	DROOPY	REFLECTIONS

Scorpions Vocabulary

DROOPY	SUBWAY	DROOPED	VAGUELY	GLANCED
MUSTY	CONTAMINATE	ACCUSATIONS	VIALS	STOCKY
JUVENILE	GLISTEN	FREE SPACE	EPISODE	STOOP
LINGERED	YACHT	SULLENLY	TENEMENTS	COMPARTMENT
REFLECTIONS	STUMBLED	BECKONED	APPEAL	SHIELD

Scorpions Vocabulary

PEER	HASTY	PROJECTS	POLLUTION	BOBBING
PIER	ANXIOUS	STRUT	AROMA	GRAVELLY
POSSESSION	SLITS	FREE SPACE	CLENCHED	BANNISTER
PAROLE	SLICK	STAMMERED	SHIELD	APPEAL
BECKONED	STUMBLED	REFLECTIONS	COMPARTMENT	TENEMENTS

Scorpions Vocabulary

VIALS	TENEMENTS	STOCKY	STAMMERED	BOBBING
DROOPED	LINGERED	SLICK	GLISTEN	SULLENLY
GRAVELLY	REFLECTIONS	FREE SPACE	STRUT	EPISODE
SUBWAY	PEER	PAROLE	AROMA	COMPARTMENT
JUVENILE	STUMBLED	SQUAT	BECKONED	CONTAMINATE

Scorpions Vocabulary

PIER	DROOPY	SLITS	BANNISTER	STOOP
APPEAL	GLANCED	ANXIOUS	SHIELD	ACCUSATIONS
DELINQUENT	YACHT	FREE SPACE	PROJECTS	HASTY
POLLUTION	MUSTY	POSSESSION	CONTAMINATE	BECKONED
SQUAT	STUMBLED	JUVENILE	COMPARTMENT	AROMA

Scorpions Vocabulary

POSSESSION	DROOPY	ANXIOUS	SULLENLY	STUMBLED
BANNISTER	ACCUSATIONS	DROOPED	STOOP	SQUAT
AROMA	COMPARTMENT	FREE SPACE	TENEMENTS	SLITS
LINGERED	VIALS	REFLECTIONS	PROJECTS	PIER
EPISODE	BOBBING	STRUT	POLLUTION	SUBWAY

Scorpions Vocabulary

PEER	GLISTEN	APPEAL	JUVENILE	CLENCHED
SLICK	CONTAMINATE	STOCKY	BECKONED	GLANCED
YACHT	SHIELD	FREE SPACE	GRAVELLY	DELINQUENT
VAGUELY	PAROLE	MUSTY	SUBWAY	POLLUTION
STRUT	BOBBING	EPISODE	PIER	PROJECTS

Scorpions Vocabulary

REFLECTIONS	DROOPY	POSSESSION	SUBWAY	SQUAT
JUVENILE	DROOPED	LINGERED	STOOP	GRAVELLY
PROJECTS	GLISTEN	FREE SPACE	ANXIOUS	BOBBING
POLLUTION	AROMA	STOCKY	DELINQUENT	TENEMENTS
BECKONED	VAGUELY	GLANCED	PEER	STRUT

Scorpions Vocabulary

PAROLE	PIER	VIALS	SLITS	STUMBLED
CLENCHED	ACCUSATIONS	STAMMERED	COMPARTMENT	HASTY
YACHT	EPISODE	FREE SPACE	SLICK	BANNISTER
SHIELD	APPEAL	MUSTY	STRUT	PEER
GLANCED	VAGUELY	BECKONED	TENEMENTS	DELINQUENT

Scorpions Vocabulary

CLENCHED	CONTAMINATE	SUBWAY	YACHT	SLICK
BECKONED	PIER	PROJECTS	ANXIOUS	DROOPY
STOCKY	VAGUELY	FREE SPACE	POLLUTION	BANNISTER
STRUT	STOOP	AROMA	REFLECTIONS	MUSTY
COMPARTMENT	BOBBING	DELINQUENT	DROOPED	SQUAT

Scorpions Vocabulary

HASTY	VIALS	SULLENLY	EPISODE	POSSESSION
GLANCED	PAROLE	STAMMERED	GRAVELLY	GLISTEN
APPEAL	TENEMENTS	FREE SPACE	PEER	ACCUSATIONS
SHIELD	LINGERED	STUMBLED	SQUAT	DROOPED
DELINQUENT	BOBBING	COMPARTMENT	MUSTY	REFLECTIONS

Scorpions Vocabulary

GLANCED	BECKONED	DELINQUENT	PAROLE	LINGERED
SQUAT	VIALS	CONTAMINATE	DROOPED	HASTY
MUSTY	EPISODE	FREE SPACE	STOOP	SHIELD
BANNISTER	SLICK	AROMA	PEER	TENEMENTS
STOCKY	GLISTEN	GRAVELLY	STAMMERED	POLLUTION

Scorpions Vocabulary

POSSESSION	ANXIOUS	YACHT	CLENCHED	REFLECTIONS
PROJECTS	SULLENLY	BOBBING	COMPARTMENT	SUBWAY
ACCUSATIONS	STUMBLED	FREE SPACE	PIER	APPEAL
VAGUELY	SLITS	DROOPY	POLLUTION	STAMMERED
GRAVELLY	GLISTEN	STOCKY	TENEMENTS	PEER

Scorpions Vocabulary

SULLENLY	TENEMENTS	BANNISTER	LINGERED	ANXIOUS
SLICK	STOOP	AROMA	MUSTY	PROJECTS
GLISTEN	DELINQUENT	FREE SPACE	CLENCHED	GRAVELLY
VIALS	STOCKY	APPEAL	STUMBLED	DROOPED
SQUAT	EPISODE	PAROLE	JUVENILE	PIER

Scorpions Vocabulary

STAMMERED	DROOPY	COMPARTMENT	POLLUTION	STRUT
SLITS	VAGUELY	GLANCED	ACCUSATIONS	YACHT
CONTAMINATE	REFLECTIONS	FREE SPACE	POSSESSION	BOBBING
SHIELD	PEER	HASTY	PIER	JUVENILE
PAROLE	EPISODE	SQUAT	DROOPED	STUMBLED

Scorpions Vocabulary

DROOPED	MUSTY	CONTAMINATE	POLLUTION	LINGERED
PEER	JUVENILE	SULLENLY	DELINQUENT	STAMMERED
GLISTEN	BOBBING	FREE SPACE	STOOP	PIER
HASTY	SLITS	REFLECTIONS	STUMBLED	SUBWAY
EPISODE	SLICK	GLANCED	ACCUSATIONS	SQUAT

Scorpions Vocabulary

YACHT	BANNISTER	GRAVELLY	APPEAL	VAGUELY
CLENCHED	STOCKY	TENEMENTS	BECKONED	ANXIOUS
STRUT	AROMA	FREE SPACE	PROJECTS	POSSESSION
VIALS	DROOPY	COMPARTMENT	SQUAT	ACCUSATIONS
GLANCED	SLICK	EPISODE	SUBWAY	STUMBLED

Scorpions Vocabulary

LINGERED	EPISODE	COMPARTMENT	SLICK	HASTY
STUMBLED	SQUAT	MUSTY	BANNISTER	GRAVELLY
GLANCED	PEER	FREE SPACE	ANXIOUS	STAMMERED
CLENCHED	APPEAL	SUBWAY	AROMA	VIALS
TENEMENTS	DROOPY	BECKONED	DROOPED	STOCKY

Scorpions Vocabulary

PIER	REFLECTIONS	SULLENLY	STOOP	CONTAMINATE
YACHT	VAGUELY	SLITS	DELINQUENT	BOBBING
POLLUTION	ACCUSATIONS	FREE SPACE	STRUT	PAROLE
PROJECTS	GLISTEN	POSSESSION	STOCKY	DROOPED
BECKONED	DROOPY	TENEMENTS	VIALS	AROMA

Scorpions Vocabulary

TENEMENTS	STOOP	COMPARTMENT	DELINQUENT	GLANCED
STRUT	CLENCHED	PAROLE	ACCUSATIONS	ANXIOUS
STAMMERED	SLITS	FREE SPACE	DROOPY	CONTAMINATE
POLLUTION	LINGERED	MUSTY	DROOPED	PEER
HASTY	YACHT	EPISODE	BECKONED	GLISTEN

Scorpions Vocabulary

REFLECTIONS	AROMA	VAGUELY	STOCKY	SULLENLY
BANNISTER	GRAVELLY	VIALS	POSSESSION	SHIELD
PIER	PROJECTS	FREE SPACE	BOBBING	SLICK
JUVENILE	SUBWAY	STUMBLED	GLISTEN	BECKONED
EPISODE	YACHT	HASTY	PEER	DROOPED

Scorpions Vocabulary

APPEAL	GLISTEN	MUSTY	GLANCED	STUMBLED
PAROLE	PEER	CLENCHED	POSSESSION	CONTAMINATE
SQUAT	SHIELD	FREE SPACE	SLICK	BANNISTER
REFLECTIONS	BECKONED	SLITS	JUVENILE	BOBBING
ACCUSATIONS	STOOP	VIALS	COMPARTMENT	TENEMENTS

Scorpions Vocabulary

PIER	YACHT	STOCKY	POLLUTION	SULLENLY
ANXIOUS	DROOPED	PROJECTS	STRUT	SUBWAY
HASTY	LINGERED	FREE SPACE	VAGUELY	STAMMERED
DELINQUENT	AROMA	EPISODE	TENEMENTS	COMPARTMENT
VIALS	STOOP	ACCUSATIONS	BOBBING	JUVENILE

Scorpions Vocabulary

PAROLE	REFLECTIONS	DROOPY	TENEMENTS	STUMBLED
GRAVELLY	VIALS	YACHT	BOBBING	MUSTY
BECKONED	STOOP	FREE SPACE	POLLUTION	SHIELD
STOCKY	SLICK	LINGERED	GLANCED	DROOPED
AROMA	PIER	APPEAL	CONTAMINATE	PEER

Scorpions Vocabulary

ANXIOUS	SQUAT	STAMMERED	STRUT	BANNISTER
GLISTEN	VAGUELY	SLITS	HASTY	JUVENILE
ACCUSATIONS	SUBWAY	FREE SPACE	CLENCHED	DELINQUENT
COMPARTMENT	EPISODE	SULLENLY	PEER	CONTAMINATE
APPEAL	PIER	AROMA	DROOPED	GLANCED

Scorpions Vocabulary

AROMA	SUBWAY	BOBBING	APPEAL	STAMMERED
VIALS	PEER	ACCUSATIONS	REFLECTIONS	GRAVELLY
ANXIOUS	STOOP	FREE SPACE	GLANCED	SULLENLY
LINGERED	DROOPED	STRUT	STOCKY	YACHT
SQUAT	MUSTY	SLICK	STUMBLED	SLITS

Scorpions Vocabulary

TENEMENTS	GLISTEN	EPISODE	CONTAMINATE	BANNISTER
JUVENILE	BECKONED	PAROLE	SHIELD	PIER
DELINQUENT	VAGUELY	FREE SPACE	HASTY	DROOPY
POLLUTION	PROJECTS	CLENCHED	SLITS	STUMBLED
SLICK	MUSTY	SQUAT	YACHT	STOCKY

www.ingramcontent.com/pod-product-compliance
Lightning Source LLC
LaVergne TN
LVHW081538060526
838200LV00048B/2129

9 781602 494008